Eunice Carey
1935

THE FACTS ABOUT SHAKESPEARE

THE MACMILLAN COMPANY
NEW YORK · BOSTON · CHICAGO · DALLAS
ATLANTA · SAN FRANCISCO

MACMILLAN & CO., LIMITED
LONDON · BOMBAY · CALCUTTA
MELBOURNE

THE MACMILLAN COMPANY
OF CANADA, LIMITED
TORONTO

The Shakespeare Monument in the Parish Church,
Stratford-on-Avon.

THE FACTS ABOUT SHAKESPEARE

BY

WILLIAM ALLAN NEILSON

AND

ASHLEY HORACE THORNDIKE

Revised Edition

New York

THE MACMILLAN COMPANY

1933

Set up and electrotyped. Published November, 1913. Reprinted April, 1914; July, 1915; May, November, 1916; January, 1918; February, September, 1920; September, 1921; March, 1922; February, December, 1923; October, 1924; June, 1926; January, December, 1927; October, 1929.
Revised edition, October, 1931. Reprinted April, 1933; October, 1933.

SET UP AND ELECTROTYPED BY J. S. CUSHING CO.
PRINTED IN THE UNITED STATES OF AMERICA
BY BERWICK & SMITH CO.

Contents

THE FACTS ABOUT SHAKESPEARE

The Facts about Shakespeare

CHAPTER I

SHAKESPEARE'S ENGLAND AND LONDON

SHAKESPEARE lived in a period of change. In religion, politics, literature, and commerce, in the habits of daily living, in the world of ideas, his lifetime witnessed continual change and movement. When Elizabeth came to the throne, six years before he was born, England was still largely Catholic, as it had been for nine centuries; when she died England was Protestant, and by the date of Shakespeare's death it was well on the way to becoming Puritan. The Protestant Reformation had worked nearly its full course of revolution in ideas, habits, and beliefs. The authority of the church had been replaced by that of the Bible, of the English Bible, superbly translated by Shakespeare's contemporaries. Within his lifetime, again, England had attained a national unity and an international importance heretofore unknown. The Spanish Armada had been defeated, the kingdoms of England and Scotland united, and the first colony established in America. Even more revolutionary had been the assertion of national greatness in literature and thought. The Italian Renaissance, following the rediscovery of Greek and Roman literature, had extended its influence to England early in the century, but only after the accession of Elizabeth did it bring full harvest. The names that crowd the next fifty years represent fine native endowments, boundless aspiration, and also novelty, — as Spenser in poetry, Bacon in philosophy, Hooker in theology. In commerce as well as in letters there was this same activity and innovation. It was a time of commercial pros-perity, of increase in comfort and luxury, of the growth of a powerful commercial class, of large fortunes and large benefactions. Whatever your status, your birth, trade, profession, residence, religion, education, or property, in the year 1564 you had a better chance to change these than any of your ancestors had; and there was more chance than there had ever been that your son would improve his inheritance. The individual man had long been boxed up in guild, church, or the feudal system; now the covers were opened, and the new opportunity bred daring, initiative, and ambition. The exploits of the Elizabethan sea rovers still stir us with the thrill of adventure; but adventure and vicissitude were hardly less the share of merchant, priest, poet, or politician. The individual has had no such opportunity for fame in England before or since.

The nineteenth century, which saw the industrial revolution, the triumphs of steam and electricity, and the discoveries of natural science, is the only period that equalled the Elizabethan in the rapidity of its changes in ideas and in the conditions of living; and even that era of change offered relatively fewer new impulses to individual greatness than the fifty years of Shakespeare's life.

Shakespeare's England was an agricultural country of four or five million inhabitants. It fed itself, except when poor harvests compelled the importation of grain, and it supplemented agriculture by grazing, fishing, and commerce, chiefly with the Netherlands, but growing in many directions. The forests were becoming thin, but the houses were still of timber; the roads were poor, the large towns mostly seaports. The dialects spoken were various, but the speech of the midland counties had become established in London, at the universities, and in printed books, and was rapidly increasing its dominance. The monasteries and religious orders were gone, but feudalism still held sway, and the people were divided into classes, — the various ranks of the nobility, the gentry, the yeomen, the burgesses, and the common people. But changes from one class to another were numerous; for many lords were losing their inheritances by extravagance, while many business men were putting their profits into land. In spite of persecutions, occasional insurrections, and the plague which devastated the unsanitary towns, it was a time of peace and prosperity. The coinage was reformed, roads were improved, taxes were not burdensome, and life in the country was more comfortable and secure than it had been. Books and education were spreading. Numerous grammar schools taught Latin, the universities made provision for poor students, and there were now many careers besides that of the church open to the educated man.

Stratford, then a village of some two thousand inhabitants. somewhat off the main route of traffic, was far more removed from the world than most towns of similar size in this day of railways, newspapers, and the telegraph. With the nearby country, it made up an independent community that attended to its own affairs with great thoroughness. The corporation, itself the outgrowth of a medieval religious guild, regulated the affairs of every one with little regard for personal liberty. It was especially severe on rebellious servants, idle apprentices, shrewish women, the pigs that ran loose in the streets, and (after 1605) persons guilty of profanity. Regular church attendance and fixed hours of work were required. The corporation frequently punished with fines (the poet's father on one occasion) those who did not clean the street before their houses; and it was much occupied in regulating the ale-houses, of which the village possessed some thirty. Like all towns of this period, Stratford suffered frequently from fire and the plague. Trade was dependent mainly on the weekly markets and semi-annual fairs, and Stratford was by no means isolated, being not far from the great market town of Coventry, near Kenilworth and Warwick, and only eighty miles from London.

Shakespeare's England was merry England. At least, it was probably as near to deserving that adjective as at any time before or since. There was plenty of time for amusement. There were public bowling-greens and archery butts in Stratford, though the corporation was very strict in regard to the hours when these could be used. Every one enjoyed hunting, hawking, cock-fighting, bull-baiting, dancing, until the Puritans found such enjoyments immoral. The youthful Shakespeare acquired an intimate knowledge of dogs and horses, hunting and falconry, though this was a gentleman's sport. The highways were full of ballad singers, beggars, acrobats, and wandering players. Play-acting of one kind or another had long been common over most of rural England. Miracle plays were given at Coventry up to 1580, and bands of professional actors came to Stratford frequently, and on their first recorded appearance received their permission to act from the bailiff, John Shakespeare (1568–1569). There was many a Holofernes or Bottom to marshal his pupils or fellow-mechanics for an amateur performance; and Shakespeare may have seen the most famous of the royal entertainments, that at Kenilworth in 1575, when Gascoigne recited poetry, and Leicester, impersonating Deep Desire, addressed

Elizabeth from a bush, and a minstrel represented Arion on a dolphin's back. The tradition may be right which declares that it was the trumpets of the comedians that summoned Shakespeare to London.

In the main, life in the country was not so very different from what it is now in the remoter places. Many a secluded English village, as recently as fifty years ago, jogged on much as in the sixteenth century. Opportunity then as now dwelt mostly in the cities, but the city of the sixteenth century bore slight resemblance to a city of to-day.

London, with less than 200,000 inhabitants, was still a medieval city in appearance, surrounded by a defensive wall, guarded by the Tower, and crowned by the cathedral. The city proper lay on the north of the Thames, and the wall made a semicircle of some two miles, from the Tower on the east to the Fleet ditch and Blackfriars on the west. Seven gates pierced the wall to the north, and the roads passing through them into the fields were lined with houses. Westward along the river were great palaces, behind which the building was practically continuous along the muddy road that led to the separate city of Westminster. The Thames, noted for its fish and swans, was the great thoroughfare, crowded with many kinds of boats and spanned by the famous London Bridge. By one of the many rowboats that carried passengers hither and thither, or on foot over the arches of the bridge, between the rows of houses that lined it, and under the heads of criminals which decorated its entrance, you might cross the Thames to Southwark. Turning west, past St. Saviour's and the palace of the Bishop of Winchester, you were soon on the Bankside, a locality long given over to houses of ill fame and rings for the baiting of bulls and bears. The theaters, forbidden in the city proper, were built either in the fields to the north of the walls, or across the river close by the kennels and rings. Here, as Shakespeare waited for a boatman to ferry him across to Blackfriars, the whole city was spread before his eyes, in the foreground the panorama of the beautiful river, beyond it the crowded houses, the spires of many churches, and the great tower of old St. Paul's.

It was a city of narrow streets, open sewers, wooden houses, without an adequate water supply or sanitation, in constant danger from fire and plague. But dirt and disease were no more prevalent than they had been for centuries; in spite of them, there was no lack of life in the crowded lanes. The great palaces were outside the city proper, and there were few notable buildings within its precincts except the churches. The dismantled monasteries still occupied large areas, but were being made over to strange uses, the theaters eventually finding a place in Blackfriars and Whitefriars. The Strand was an ill-paved street running behind the river palaces, past the village of Charing Cross, on to the royal palace of Whitehall and to the Abbey and Hall at Westminster. The walls and sur-

rounding moat had ceased to be of use for defense, and
building constantly spread into the fields without.
These fields were favorite places for recreation and
served the purpose of city parks. The Elizabethans
were fond of outdoor sports and spent little daytime
indoors. The shops were open to the street, and
the clear spaces at Cheapside and St. Paul's Church-
yard seem to have been always crowded. St. Paul's,
although still used for religious services, had become a
sort of city club or general meeting place. Mules and
horses were no longer to be found there as in the reign of
Mary, but the nave was in constant use as a place for
gossip and business. The churchyard was the usual
place for holding lotteries, and here were the shops of
a majority of the London booksellers. In its northeast
corner was Paul's Cross, the famous pulpit whence the
wishes of the government were announced and popular-
ized by the Sunday preachers. And here the variety
of London life was most fully exhibited. The processions and entertainments at court, the ambassadors
from afar, the law students from the Temple, the old
soldiers destitute after service in Flanders, the seamen
returned from plundering the Spanish gold fleet, the
youths from the university come to the city to earn their
living by their wits, the bishop and the puritan, who
looked at each other askance, the young squire come to
be gulled of his lands by the roarers of the tavern, the
solid merchant with his chain of gold, the wives who
aped the court ladies with their enormous farthingales

and ruffs, the court gallant with his dyed beard and huge breeches, the idle apprentices quick to riot, the poor poets in prison for debt — these and how many more are familiar to every reader of the Elizabethan drama. As often in periods of commercial prosperity, luxury became fantastic. Men sold their acres to put costly garments on their backs. Clothing was absurd and ran to extreme sizes of ruffs, farthingales, and breeches, or to gaudy colors and jewels. Enormous sums were spent on feasts, entertainments, and masques, especially in the reign of James I. Cleanliness did not thrive, perfumes took the place of baths, and rushes, seldom renewed, covered the floor even of the presence chamber of Elizabeth. But the comforts and luxuries of life increased and spread to all classes. Tobacco, potatoes, and forks were first introduced in Shakespeare's time. Building improved, streets were widened, and coaches became so common as to excite much animadversion and complaint. If some poets spent much time in the debtors' prison, others lived well, and some actors gained large fortunes.

The industrious apprentice who refused the allurements of pageants, theaters, tailors, and taverns, was sure to have his reward. It was a time of commercial expansion, such as the late nineteenth century saw in Germany and the United States. Bankers, brokers, and merchants gained great fortunes and managed to protect them. Industry, thrift, and shrewdness were likely to win enough to buy a knighthood. The trade of the old East and the new West came to the London wharves, and every one was ready to take a risk. The merchants of London had furnished support to the policies of Henry VIII and were rich enough to fit out the expedition against Flanders and to pay for a third of the fleet that met the Armada. It was a time, too, for great enterprises and benefactions to charity. Sir Thomas Gresham built the Exchange, Sir Hugh Middleton paid for the New River water supply, and there were many gifts to hospitals. With all this increase in wealth, the various professions prospered, especially that of law. The inns of court were crowded with students, not a few of whom forsook the courts for the drama. The age of chivalry was over, that of commerce begun. No one gained much glory by a military career in the days of Elizabeth. The church, the law, banking, commerce, even politics and literature, offered better roads to wealth or fame.

The importance of the court in Elizabethan London is not easy to realize to-day. It dominated the life of the small city. Its nobles and their retainers, its courtiers and hangers-on, made up a considerable portion of the population; its shows supplied the entertainment, its gossip the politics of the hour. It was the seat of pageantry, the mirror of manners, the patron or the oppressor of every one. No one could be so humble as to escape coming somehow within its sway, and some of the greatest wrecked their lives in efforts to secure its approval. It is no wonder that the plays of

Shakespeare deal so largely with kings, queens, and their courts. Under the Tudors, and still more under the Stuarts, the court aimed at increasing the central authority so as to bring every affair of its subjects under its direct control. In London, however, this effort at centralization met with strong opposition. The government was in the hands of the guilds representative of the wealth of the city, and was coming face to face with many of the problems of modern municipalities. The corporation was in constant clash with the court; and in the end the city, which had supported Henry VIII and Elizabeth against powerful nobles, became the Puritan London that aided in ousting the Stuarts.

This conflict between city and court is illustrated in the regulation of the theaters and companies of actors. The actors had a legal status only as the license of some nobleman enrolled them as his servants, and they relied on the protection of their patron and the court against the opposition of the city authorities. The fact that they were employed to give plays before the Queen was, indeed, about the only argument that won any consideration from the corporation. This opposition was based in part on moral or puritan grounds, but was determined still more by the fear of three menaces, fire, sedition, and the plague. Wooden buildings were already discouraged by statute, and the danger of fire from the wooden theaters is shown by the burning of the Globe and the Fortune. The gathering of crowds was feared by every property holder, and the theaters were frequently the scenes of outbreaks of the apprentices. The danger of the plague from the crowd at plays was the greatest of all. London was hardly ever free from it, and suffered terrible devastation in the years 1593 and 1603. For these reasons the theaters were forbidden within the city's jurisdiction, and were driven into the outskirts. The best companies appeared frequently at court, and on the accession of James I they were licensed directly as servants of various members of the royal family. The actors were thereafter under the immediate control of the court, and certain "private" theaters were established within the city. But this triumph of the court over the long opposition of the city was not an unmixed blessing for the drama.

The theaters in 1590 represented the public on which they depended for support; by 1616 they were far less representative of the nation or London, and more dependent on the court and its following. The Blackfriars theater, before which gathered the crowd of coaches that annoyed the puritans of the neighborhood, was a symptom of the growth of wealth and luxury, and of the increased power of the monarchy; the protests of the puritan neighborhood were an indication of the growth of a large class hostile alike to an arbitrary court, luxury, and the theater.

Shakespeare's lifetime, however, saw little of this sharp division into parties or of that narrow moral

consistency which Puritanism came to require. Looking back on his age in contrast with our own, we are
perhaps most impressed by its striking incongruities.
This London of dirt and disease was also the arena for
extravagant fashion and princely display. This popu-
lace that watched with joy the cruel torment of a bear
or the execution of a Catholic also delighted in the
romantic comedies of Shakespeare. This people, so
appallingly credulous and ignorant, so brutal, childish,
so mercurial compared with Englishmen of to-day,
yet set the standard of national greatness. This
absurdly decorated gallant could stab a rival in the
back or write a penitential lyric. Each man presents
strange, almost inexplicable, contrasts in character,
as Bacon or Raleigh, or Elizabeth herself. The drama
mingles its sentiment and fancy with horrors and
bloodshed; and no wonder, for poetry was no occupation of the cloister. Read the lives of the poets —
Surrey, Wyatt, Sidney, Spenser, Raleigh, Marlowe,
Jonson — and of these, only Spenser and Jonson died
in their beds, and Ben had killed his man in a duel.
The student of Elizabethan history and biography will
find stranger contrasts than in the lives of these poets,
for crime, meanness, and sexual depravity often appear
in the closest juxtaposition with imaginative idealism,
intellectual freedom, and moral grandeur.

The Italian Renaissance, with its mingled passions
for beauty, art, blood, lust, and intellect, seems for a
time transferred to London and dwelling alongside

of commerce and Puritanism. Yet these incongruities of character, manners, and motives that seem so striking to us to-day may probably be explained by conditions already described. The opportunities created by the changes in church and religion, the new education and prosperity, the new America, and the revived classics, all tended to create a new thirst for experience. This thirst for experience led to excess and incongruity, but it also furnished an unparalleled range of human motive for a poet's observation and imitation.

In the wide range of our poet's survey, there is, however, one notable omission. The reign of Elizabeth, like those of her three predecessors, was one of religious controversy, change, and persecution. But all this strife, all this debate, repression, persecution, and all of this great turmoil working in the minds of Englishmen, find little reflection in Shakespeare's plays, and little in the whole Elizabethan drama. Religious controversy had played a part in the drama of the reigns of Edward and Mary, but it rarely enters the Elizabethan drama, and then mainly in the form of ridicule for the puritan. Shakespeare's plays seem almost to ignore the most momentous facts of his time. They treat pagan, Catholic, and Protestant with cordiality and only smile at the puritan or Brownist. His England of the merry wives or Falstaff's justices seems strangely untroubled by questions of faith or ritual. There is, to be sure, plenty of religion and controversy in the literature of the time, but the drama as a whole is singularly non-religious. It reflects rather that freedom from restraint, that buoyancy of spirit, that lively interest in experience, which had their full course in the few years when the old garment was off and the new not quite fitted. The immense intellectual and imaginative activity of the period consists precisely in this freedom from restrictions, partisanship, dogmas, or caste. Things had lost their labels, and some time and argument were required to find new ones. Ideas were free and not bound to any school, party, or cause. You grasped an idea without knowing whether it made you realist, romanticist, or classicist; papist, puritan, or pagan. After centuries of imprisonment, individuality had its full chance in the world of ideas as elsewhere.

In a few years this was all over, and your sphere of life and the ideas proper to that sphere were prescribed for you. By another century, England had fought out the issues of creed and government with expense of blood and spirit, and had settled down to the compromise of 1688. In Shakespeare's day there was also, of course, some movement toward fixity of ideas, and there were great men who strove to convert others to their ideas and to dictate belief and conduct. But there was a breathing spell in which, comparatively speaking, men were not alike, but individual, and in which their motives and ideas revelled in a freedom from ancient precedent. In this era of flux the modern drama found its panorama of novel and varied experience making and marring character.

Shakespeare lived peaceably in the heyday of this change, nearly of an age with Sidney, Raleigh, Spenser, Bacon, Marlowe. Like Marlowe in the soliloquies of Barabbas and Faust, he recognized the new possibilities that the age opened through money or ideas. He made much out of the commercial prosperity of the day, gained such profits as were possible from his profession, raised his estate, and acquired wealth. He gave his mind not to any cause or party but to the study of men. The drunkards of the London inn, the yokels of Warwickshire, and the finest gentlewomen of the land alike came under the scrutiny of the creator of Falstaff, Dogberry, and Rosalind. And like his great contemporaries, he triumphed over incongruities, for he translated his studies of the human mind into verse of immortal beauty that yet delighted the public stage which was located halfway between the bear dens and the brothels.

CHAPTER II

BIOGRAPHICAL FACTS AND TRADITIONS

IN the time of Shakespeare, the fashion of writing lives of men of letters had not yet arisen. The art of biography could hardly be said to be even in its infancy, for the most notable early examples, such as the lives of Wolsey by Cavendish and of Sir Thomas More by his son-in-law in the sixteenth century, and Walton's handful in the seventeenth, are far from what the present age regards as scientific biography. The preservation of official records makes it possible for the modern scholar to reconstruct with considerable fullness the careers of public men; but in the case of Shakespeare, as of others of his profession, we must needs be content with a few scrappy documents, supplemented by oral traditions of varying degrees of authenticity. About Shakespeare himself it must be allowed that we have been able to learn more than about most of his fellow dramatists and actors.

In a matter which has been the subject of so much controversy, it may be an aid to clearness if the facts established by contemporary documents be first related, and the less trustworthy reports added later. The first indubitable item is trivial and unsavory enough. In

April, 1552, a certain John Shakespeare, residing in Henley Street, Stratford-on-Avon, in the county of Warwick, was fined twelvepence for failing to remove a heap of filth from before his door. This John, who shared his surname with a multitude of other Shakespeares in the England and especially in the Warwickshire of his time, appears, without reasonable doubt, to have been the father of the poet. He is described as a glover and in later tradition as a butcher; the truth seems to be that he did a miscellaneous business in farm products. For twenty years or more after this first record he prospered, rising through various petty municipal offices to the position of bailiff, or mayor, of the town in 1568. His fortunes must have been notably improved by his marriage, for the Mary Arden whom he wedded in 1557 was the daughter of a well-to-do farmer, Robert Arden, who bequeathed her £6 13s. 4d. in money and a house with fifty acres of land.

To John and Mary Shakespeare was born a son William, whose baptism was registered in the Church of the Holy Trinity in Stratford on April 26, 1564. He was their eldest son, two daughters previously born being already dead. Their other children were Gilbert, Joan, Anna, Richard, and Edmund. The precise day of William's birth is unknown. The monument over his grave states that at his death on April 23, 1616, he was "Ætatis 53," which would seem to indicate that he must have been born at least as early as April 22; and, since in those days baptism usually took place

within a very few days of birth, there is no reason for
pushing the date farther back.

Of the education of the poet we have no record.
Stratford had a free grammar school, to which such
a boy as the bailiff's son would be sure to be sent; and
the inference that William Shakespeare was a pupil
there and studied the usual Latin authors is entirely
reasonable. About 1577 his father began to get into
financial difficulties, and it is reported that about
this time the boy was withdrawn from school to help
in his father's business. We know nothing certainly,
however, until we learn from the registry of the Bishop
of Worcester that on November 28, 1582, two husband-
men of Stratford gave bonds "to defend and save harm-
less" the bishop and his officers for licensing the marriage of William Shakespeare and Anne Hathaway.
Of the actual marriage there is no record. Anne is
probably to be identified with Agnes or Anne, the
daughter of Richard Hathaway of the neighboring
hamlet of Shottery, who had died in the previous July,
and had owned the house of which a part still survives
and is shown to visitors as "Anne Hathaway's cottage."
The date on Anne's tombstone indicates that she was
eight years older than the poet.

A comparison of the bond just mentioned with other
documents of the kind indicates it to be exceptional in the
absence of any mention of consent by the bridegroom's
parents, a circumstance rendered still more remarkable
by the fact that he was a minor. The bondsmen were

from Shottery, and this, along with the considerations
already advanced, has naturally led to the inference
that the marriage was hurried by the bride's friends,
and to the finding of a motive for their haste in the
birth within six months of "Susanna, daughter to
William Shakespere," who was baptized on May 26,
1583.

The record of the baptism of Shakespeare's only
other children, the twins Hamnet and Judith, in
February, 1585, practically exhausts the documentary
evidence concerning the poet in Stratford until 1596.
It is conjectured, but not known, that about 1586 he
found his way to London and soon became connected
with the theater, according to one tradition, as call-boy,
to another, as holder of the horses of theatergoers.
But by 1592 we are assured that he had entered the
ranks of the playwrights, and had achieved enough
success to rouse the jealous resentment of a rival.
Robert Greene, who died on the third of September in
that year, left unpublished a pamphlet, *Greenes Groatsworth of Witte: bought with a Million of Repentaunce*,
in which he warned three of his fellows against certain
plagiarists, "those puppits, I meane, that speake from
our mouths, those anticks garnisht in our colours."
"Yes, trust them not," he goes on; "for there is an
upstart crow, beautified with our feathers, that with
his *Tygers heart wrapt in a Players hide*, supposes he is
as well able to bumbast out a blanke verse as the best
of you; and being an absolute *Johannes Factotum*, is

in his owne conceit the only Shake-scene in a countrie.
O that I might intreate your rare wits to be imployed
in more profitable courses, and let those apes imitate
your past excellence, and never more acquaint them
with your admired inventions! I know the best
husband of you all will never prove an usurer, and the
kindest of them all wil never proove a kinde nurse; yet,
whilst you may, seeke you better maisters, for it is pittie
men of such rare wits should be subject to the pleas-
ures of such rude groomes." The phrase about the
"tyger's heart" is an obvious parody on the line,

> Oh Tiger's heart wrapt in a woman's hide!

which occurs both in *The True Tragedie of Richard Duke
of Yorke*, and in the variant of that play which is
included in the First Folio as the third part of *Henry VI*.
"The only Shake-scene" has naturally been taken as
an allusion to Shakespeare's name; and it is scarcely
possible to doubt the reference to him throughout the
passage. This being so, we may infer that by this date
Shakespeare had written, with whatever else, his share
in the three parts of *Henry VI*, and was successful
enough to seem formidable to the dying Greene. It
is noteworthy, too, that thus early we have allusion
to his double profession: as an actor in the words
"player's hide" and "Shake-scene," and as an author
in the charge of plagiarism. That the reference in
"beautified with our feathers" is to literary plagiarism
is confirmed by the following lines from *Greene's Funer-*

alls, by R. B., 1594, which seem to have been suggested by Greene's phrase:

> Greene is the ground of everie painters die;
> Greene gave the ground to all that wrote upon him.
> Nay, more, the men that so eclipst his fame,
> *Purloynde his plumes:* can they deny the same?

Somewhat less certain is the allusion in a document closely connected with the foregoing. *Greenes Groatsworth* had been prepared for the press by his friend Henry Chettle, and in the address "To the Gentlemen Readers" prefixed to his *Kind-Harts Dreame* (registered December 8, 1592), Chettle regrets that he has not struck out from Greene's book the passages that have been "offensively by one or two of them taken." "With neither of them that take offence was I acquainted, and with one of them I care not if I never be. The other, whome at that time I did not so much spare as since I wish I had, for that as I have moderated the heate of living writers, and might have usde my owne discretion, — especially in such a case, the Author beeing dead, — that I did not, I am as sorry, as if the originall fault had beene my fault, because myselfe have seene his demeanor no lesse civill, than he exelent in the qualitie[1] he professes: Besides, divers of worship have reported his uprightnes of dealing, which argues his honesty, and his facetious grace in writing, that

---

[1] *I.e.*, profession, used especially at that time of the profession of acting.

aprooves his Art." This characterization so well fits in with the tone of later contemporary allusions to Shakespeare that it is regrettable that Chettle did not make its reference to him beyond a doubt.

Within a few months after the disturbance caused by Greene's charges, Shakespeare appeared in the field of authorship in quite unambiguous fashion. On April 18, 1593, Richard Field, himself a Stratford man, entered at Stationers' Hall a book entitled *Venus and Adonis*. The dedication, which is to the Earl of Southampton, is signed by "William Shakespeare," and the state of the text confirms the inference that the poet himself oversaw the publication. The terms of the dedication, read in the light of contemporary examples of this kind of writing, do not imply any close relation between poet and patron; and the phrase "the first heyre of my invention," applied to the poem, need not be taken as placing its composition earlier than any of the plays, since writing for the stage was then scarcely regarded as practising the art of letters. *Lucrece* was registered May 9, 1594, and appeared likewise without a name on the title-page, but with Shakespeare's full signature attached to a dedication, somewhat more warmly personal than before, to the same nobleman. The frequency of complimentary references to these poems, and the number of editions issued during the poet's lifetime (seven of *Venus*, and five of *Lucrece*), indicate that it was through them that he first obtained literary distinction.

Meanwhile he was gaining a footing as an actor. The accounts of the Treasurer of the Chamber for March 15, 1594–5, bear record of Shakespeare's having been summoned, along with Kempe and Burbage, as a member of the Lord Chamberlain's Company, to present two comedies before the Queen at Greenwich Palace in the Christmas season of 1594. This is the earliest mention of the poet as sharing with his company a kind of recognition as honorable as it was profitable.

The records now take us back to his family. On August 11, 1596, his only son Hamnet was buried. In the same year John Shakespeare applied to the College of Heralds for a grant of arms, basing the claim on services of his ancestors to Henry VII, the continued good reputation of the family, and John's marriage to "Mary, daughter and heiress of Robert Arden, of Wilmcote, gent." Since there is evidence to show that the son was by this time prospering in London, and since the attempts of actors to obtain gentility by grants of arms were not uncommon, it is likely that the poet was the moving force in this matter. Two drafts granting this request are preserved in Heralds' College, London, one dated October 20, 1596; and a third draft confirming and extending the grant is dated 1599. The coat of arms is described as follows : "Or [gold], on a bend sable a spear of the first, the point argent; and for the crest, a falcon, argent, with his wings displayed, supporting a spear in pale; Or [gold], the point argent, standing on a wreath of his colours and provided with a

helmet, mantle and tassels according to custom." The
motto is "Non Sans Droit." These arms appear on
the monument over Shakespeare's grave in Trinity
Church in Stratford, and, impaled with the Hall arms,
on the tombstone of his daughter Susanna and her husband John Hall.

A more substantial step towards restoring the
standing of the family was taken when the poet bought
on May 4, 1597, for sixty pounds, New Place, the
largest house in Stratford. This was only the beginning
of a considerable series of investments of the profits of
his professional life in landed and other property in his
native district. On his father's death in 1601 he in-
herited the two houses in Henley Street, the only real
property of which the elder Shakespeare had retained
possession; and in one of these the poet's mother lived
until her death in 1608. About a hundred and seven
acres of arable land with common pasture appertaining
to it was conveyed to the poet on May 1, 1602, by William and John Combe, of Warwick and Old Stratford
respectively, in consideration of £320; and twenty
acres of pasture land were acquired from the same
owners in 1610. On September 28, 1602, the Court
Rolls of the Manor of Rowington record the transfer to
Shakespeare from Walter Getley of a cottage and
garden in Chapel Lane, Stratford. In 1605 he paid
£440 for the thirty-one years remaining of a lease of a
portion of the Stratford tithes, a purchase which involved him in considerable litigation. It was through

this acquisition that he became involved in the dispute over the attempted inclosure of certain common fields belonging to the town of Stratford. John Combe, who died in July, 1614, bequeathing Shakespeare £5, left as heir a son, William, who with Arthur Mannering, sought to annex to their respective estates the aforesaid common lands. After having secured a deed safeguarding himself as part owner of the tithes from any loss that might result from the inclosure, Shakespeare seems to have lent his influence to Combe, in spite of the requests of the corporation for aid. The inclosure was not carried out.

His investments were not confined to his native county. A deed of sale has come down to us concerning the purchase of a house near the Blackfriars Theater in London, in March, 1613. The price was £140; but on the following day, March 11, Shakespeare gave the previous owner, Henry Walker, a mortgage deed for £60. He probably paid off this mortgage, for in his will he bequeathed this property to his daughter Susanna. Three documents, discovered by Professor C. W. Wallace, and dated April 26, May 15, and May 22, 1615, deal with a suit in Chancery, in which Shakespeare and others sought to obtain from one Mathias Bacon possession of certain deeds pertaining to their property within the precinct of Blackfriars.

Other traces of Shakespeare's business transactions suggest that he was by no means averse to going to law. After his resumption of relations with Stratford in

1596, we find his parents engaged (November, 1597) in a lawsuit, the outcome of which does not appear, to recover the mortgaged estate of Asbies, which had formed part of his mother's inheritance. The years 1600, 1604, 1608, and 1609 all contain records of suits by the poet to recover small sums of money; and, on the other hand, we find tax collectors in London seeking payment of taxes incurred on his goods while he lived in the parish of St. Helen's, Bishopgate, in 1593 or 1594. These claims Shakespeare satisfied some years later when he was living across the river in Southwark. The documents of a law case of 1612, recently discovered by Professor C. W. Wallace in the Public Record office, include Shakespeare's deposition as a witness and add some interesting information. It appears that, possibly from 1602 to 1604, he lodged in the house of Christopher Mountjoy, a wigmaker, at the corner of Muggle and Silver streets near Cripplegate. In 1604 he had aided in arranging the marriage of Mary Mountjoy to her father's apprentice, Stephen Bellott. The lawsuit was brought by Bellott against his father-in-law to secure the dowry and promise of inheritance. Shakespeare's negotiations in regard to the marriage play an important part in the various depositions, as the question what, if any, dowry had been promised was crucial to the case. Shakespeare himself was examined on September 11, but the poet failed to remember what definite sum had been agreed upon for the dowry.

Further evidence relating to Shakespeare as a man of substance is to be found in letters in the Stratford archives, written by prominent townsmen. One, from Abraham Sturley to a relative in London on the business of the town of Stratford, dated January 24, 1597–8, contains a reference to "Mr. Shaksper" as "willing to disburse some money upon some odd yardland or other at Shottery or near about us," and suggests urging upon Shakespeare the purchase of the tithes. It seems fairly certain from other letters of Sturley's that this one was addressed to Richard Quiney, father of Shakespeare's future son-in-law, Thomas Quiney. On October 25 of the same year, this Richard Quiney wrote from the Bell in Carter Lane, London, "to my loving good friend and countryman, Mr. Wm. Shackespere," asking for his help with £30. From a letter from Abraham Sturley to Richard Quiney on the following fourth of November it appears that Quiney was seeking an enlargement of the charter of Stratford, with a view to an increase of revenue. In Sturley's previous letter reference had been made to an attempt to gain "an ease and discharge of such taxes and subsidies wherewith our town is like to be charged, and I assure you I am in great fear and doubt by no means able to pay." In this extreme condition of affairs Sturley heard with satisfaction "that our countryman Mr. Wm. Shak. would procure us money, which I will like of as I shall hear when, and where, and how; and I pray let not go that occasion if it may sort to any indifferent conditions." The poet is probably referred to in still another letter, of about the same period, to Richard Quiney, this time from his father Adrian: "If you bargain with Wm. Sha., or receive money therefor, bring your money home if you may." All of these documents carry the unmistakable implication that William Shakespeare in London was regarded by his fellow-townsmen as a person of resources, likely to be of service to his friends in financial stress.

If we return now to the evidences of Shakespeare's professional progress, we shall see whence these resources were derived. Confining ourselves still to explicit and unambiguous records, we find the year 1598 marking Shakespeare's emergence as actor and dramatist into a somewhat opener publicity. The quarto editions of *Richard II* and *Love's Labour's Lost,* issued that year, are the first plays to exhibit his name on the title-page; and in the 1616 folio edition of Ben Jonson's works, attached to *Every Man in His Humour,* is the statement: "This Comedie was first Acted in the yeere 1598 by the then L. Chamberleyne his servants. The principal Comedians were Will. Shakespeare, Aug. Philips, Hen. Condel, Will. Slye, Will. Kempe, Ric. Burbadge, Joh. Hemings, Tho. Pope, Chr. Beeston, Joh. Dyke." These evidences of prominence are more than corroborated by the famous passage in the *Palladis Tamia* (1598) of Francis Meres, in which he not only compares the "mellifluous and honey-tongued Shakespeare" with Ovid for his *Venus and Adonis*, his *Lucrece*, "his sugred sonnets among his private friends," but with Plautus and Seneca for his excellence "in both kinds for the stage; for comedy, witness his Gentlemen of Verona, his Errors, his Love Labors Lost, his Love Labours Wonne, his Midsummers Night Dreame, and his Merchant of Venice; for tragedy, his Richard the 2, Richard the 3, Henry the 4, King John, Titus Andronicus, and his Romeo and Juliet." Barnfield in the same year harps on the "honey-flowing vein" of the author of *Venus* and *Lucrece*, and "honey-tongued" is again the opening epithet of John Weever's epigram "Ad Gulielmum Shakespeare" (1599), in which "*Romeo*" and "*Richard*" share the praises with the narrative poems. From this time on, publishers of the plays recognize Shakespeare's reputation by generally placing his name on the title-page: a form of compliment which the author probably did not appreciate when it was extended, as in the case of *The Passionate Pilgrim* (1599), to pirated works, some of which were meant to be private, and others were not by him at all.

Reminiscences or references to his works are frequent in contemporary literature. Among these are several passages in two plays, *The Return from Parnassus*, acted in St. John's College, Cambridge, about 1601. In one passage, Kempe, the famous actor, speaks slightingly of the acting qualities of the plays by university pens and continues, "Why here's our fellow Shakespeare puts them all down, ay, and Ben Jonson too," —

another identification of the actor and the dramatist Shakespeare. Another character in these plays classes Shakespeare with Chaucer, Gower, and Spenser. Less enthusiastic though sincerely appreciative is John Webster, who, in the address to the Reader prefixed to *The White Devil*, 1612, acknowledges his indebtedness to his predecessors, Chapman, Jonson, Beaumont, and Fletcher and to "the right happy and copious industry of Master Shakespeare, Master Dekker, and Master Heywood." Though of widely varying significance and interest, the numerous allusions to Shakespeare or to his plays give further testimony to his growing reputation.

While it is probable that the sale of Shakespeare's poems brought him in some financial return, he is not likely to have profited from the publication of his plays. The playwright at that time sold his product to the manager or company, and thereby gave up all rights. To the end of the sixteenth century the manager Henslowe paid from £5 to £11 for a new play, but a little later the price had risen to £20. Shakespeare, however, was in an unusual position as a dramatist in that he wrote solely for one company of actors in which he was a shareholder. Moreover, this company was the best managed and most prosperous of all. Probably he received larger payments for his plays than did Henslowe's hackwriters; at all events his company must have given some considerable financial reward for the plays which rapidly became the most valuable portion of its

repertory._ Whatever salary he received as playwright
or as actor, he shared in the special payments for court
performances and in the profits of the company. In
1635 an actor-shareholder's profit was estimated at £90.

Even more substantial might be the annual profits of a
sharer in the ownership or lease of the playhouses. In
the company of which Burbage was the chief actor and
Shakespeare the chief dramatist, the leading members
were both "shareholders" in the profits of the company
and "householders" or sharers in the profits of the playhouse. Later on, those whose income was confined to
the former source took legal measures to secure partnership in the leases as well. In 1599 Shakespeare became
a sharer, with Heming, Condell, Philips, and others,
in the receipts of the Globe Theater, erected in 1598-9
by Richard and Cuthbert Burbage. His share was at
first one-tenth but was altered as others were added to
the sharers. In 1608 he became a sharer to the extent
of one-seventh in the smaller but profitable Blackfriars
Theater, after its lease had been acquired by the Burbages. Shakespeare's theatrical income was thus derived from various sources : payments as actor and playwright, shares in the profits of the company, rewards
for court performances, perquisites after 1603 as member
of the King's household, and shares in the profits of two
theaters. His income would vary greatly from year to
year, and for a prosperous year might come nearer to
Sir Sidney Lee's estimate of £700 than that of £200 set
by Sir Edmund K. Chambers.

The evidence thus accumulated of Shakespeare's having acquired a substantial fortune is corroborated by what we know of the earnings of other members of his profession, and it leaves no mystery about the source of the capital which he invested in real property in Stratford and London.

The death of Elizabeth and the accession of James I improved rather than impaired Shakespeare's prospects. A patent, dated May 17, 1603, licenses the King's servants, "Lawrence Fletcher, William Shakespeare, Richard Burbage . . . and the rest of their associats." By this document the Lord Chamberlain's Company became the King's, and so remained during the rest of Shakespeare's connection with the stage. They acted at court more often than any other company; in one season, that of 1610–11, presenting as many as fifteen plays, for which they received £150. On the occasion of a performance before the court at the Earl of Pembroke's mansion of Wilton House, £30 was given them "by way of his majesty's reward." Shakespeare's name stands first in a list of nine actors who walked in a procession on the occasion of James's entry into London, March 15, 1604, when each actor was granted four yards and a half of scarlet cloth for cloaks for the occasion.

This recognition by the court is the latest evidence we have of Shakespeare's belonging to the profession of acting. He is mentioned in the Jonson Folio of 1616 as playing a part in *Sejanus* in 1603; but his name

is absent from the list of the King's servants, as his
company had now become, when they performed
Volpone in 1605, *The Alchemist* in 1610, and *Catiline*
in 1611. It would thus seem that he gave up acting
shortly after the death of Elizabeth.

The date of his withdrawal from London to Stratford
is less precisely indicated. The likelihood is that the
transference was gradual; for after 1611, the date
usually conjectured for his retirement from the metrop-
olis, we have indications of at least occasional activi-
ties there, as in the collaboration with Fletcher, now
generally admitted, in *Henry VIII* and *The Two Noble
Kinsmen*, and in the business dealings in Blackfriars
already described. On the other hand, he had disposed
of his shares in the theaters before his death; as we
have seen, he appears frequently in his last years
in connection with municipal affairs in Stratford;
and later formal references are usually to "William
Shakespeare, gent., of Stratford-on-Avon." It was
during this period that we find a record of the poet as
serving in a new capacity. There has been discovered
in the Household Book at Belvoir Castle the following
entry: "Item 31 Martij (1613) to Mr. Shakspeare in
gold about my Lordes Impreso xliiij s. To Richard
Burbadge for paynting and making yt in gold xliiij s.
(Total) iiij ¹ⁱ viij ˢ." This means that the Earl of
Rutland, who took part in a tournament at Whitehall
on March 24, 1613, had the heraldic device for his
shield made by Shakespeare and Burbage, — Burbage,

whose skill as painter is well known, being probably responsible for the design and Shakespeare for the motto. Rutland was a friend and associate of that Earl of Southampton to whom Shakespeare had dedicated his two narrative poems.

The remaining documents are chiefly domestic. On June 5, 1607, his elder daughter Susanna married John Hall, a physician of Stratford, who succeeded the poet in the occupancy of New Place; and on September 9, 1608, the Stratford Register records the burial of his mother, "Mayry Shaxspere, wydowe." His younger daughter, Judith, married Thomas Quiney on February 10, 1616, with such haste and informality as led to a decree of excommunication by the ecclesiastical court at Worcester. In the previous month Shakespeare had a draft of his will drawn up by Francis Collins, a solicitor of Warwick, and after the first sheet had been rewritten and other changes made, this much corrected draft was signed and executed on March 25. On the twenty-fifth of April the Registers show the burial of "Will. Shakespeare gent." The monument over his grave gives the day of his death as April 23 (Old Style). He was buried in the chancel of Stratford Church, and on the grave may still be read the much discussed lines:

> Good friend, for Jesus' sake forbeare
> To dig the dust enclosed heare;
> Bleste be the man that spares these stones,
> And curst be he that moves my bones.

William Hall, who visited Stratford in 1694, records the tradition that the poet himself composed the lines in a style calculated to impress sextons and prevent them from digging up his bones and throwing them into the adjacent charnel house. However this may be, the grave has remained unopened.

Seven years later, thirty-six of Shakespeare's plays were collected by two of his former colleagues of the theater, Heming and Condell, whom he had remembered in his will, and published in the famous First Folio. The preliminary documents in this volume, printed in our appendix, close significantly the contemporary records of the man, and bind together the burgess of Stratford with the actor of London and the dramatist of the world.

Of Shakespeare's handwriting nothing that can be called his with complete assurance has survived except six signatures; one to the deposition in the matter of the Mountjoy marriage; one to the deed of the house he bought in Blackfriars in 1613, one to the mortgage-deed on the same house, executed on the day after the purchase, and one on each of the three sheets of paper containing his will, the last of which has in addition the words "By me." All six are somewhat crabbed specimens of the old English style of handwriting, somewhat similar to that now used in German, and then about to be supplanted in England by the Italian or italic script. Of the many other signatures attributed to the poet, the best case for genuineness has been made

THREE AUTOGRAPH SIGNATURES WRITTEN BY SHAKESPEARE ON
THREE SHEETS OF HIS WILL

From the document now at Somerset House, London

for that in a copy of the 1603 edition of Florio's translation of Montaigne. An effort has also been made to identify as Shakespeare's the handwriting of a scene in the manuscript of the old play *Sir Thomas More;* but, although this cannot with certainty be assigned to any known dramatist, it seems clearly not Shakespeare's. The manuscripts of his plays have gone the way of all, or almost all, the autographs of the men of letters of his time, nor is it likely that future research will add materially to what we have. The exact signatures, though it is difficult to be certain of all the letters, seem to show a variation in spelling — Shakspere, or Shakspeare. His father's name appears in the records of the town in sixteen different forms, an illustration of the inconsistency in the orthography of proper names, as of other words, which was common with people of that time of greater worldly consequence and education than the poet or his father. The form of the name used in the present volume is that which has been most generally adopted.

Our knowledge of Shakespeare's personal appearance is also far from being definite. The bust on the monument in the church at Stratford was cut apparently before 1623 by a Dutch stone cutter called Gerard Janssen. It was originally colored; probably the eyes light hazel, and the hair auburn. Its crude workmanship renders it unreliable as a likeness. The frontispiece to the First Folio was engraved for that work by Martin Droeshout, who was only twenty-two years old at the time, so that he is more likely to have made it from a portrait than from memory. Other portraits have been claimed as likenesses, but none has a pedigree without a flaw. Those of most interest are the Ely Palace portrait, the Chandos portrait, the Garrick Club bust, and the Kesselstadt death-mask.

Such is the very considerable body of authenticated facts about the life of Shakespeare. Lacking though they are in intimate and personal touches, they can hardly be said to leave the main outlines of his career shadowy or mysterious. But they do not by any means exhaust the data at our disposal for forming an impression of the poet's personality. A large mass of tradition, of less than legal validity but much of it of a high degree of probability, has come down to us, the sources of which may now be detailed.

In the seventeenth century we have several biographical and critical collections in which Shakespeare figures, the most important being these: Fuller's *Worthies of England* (1662), Aubrey's *Lives of Eminent Men* (compiled 1669–1696), Phillips's *Theatrum Poetarum* (1675), and Langbaine's *English Dramatic Poets* (1691). The two last are for strictly biographical purposes negligible, though interesting as early criticism. Fuller began his work in 1643, so that he may be supposed to have had access to oral tradition from men who actually knew Shakespeare. He gives few facts, but some hints as to temperament. "Though his genius generally was jocular and inclining him to festivity, yet he could, when so disposed, be solemn and serious. . . . Many were the wit-combats betwixt him and Ben Jonson; which two I behold like a Spanish great galleon and an English man-of-war; master Jonson (like the former) was built far higher in learning; solid, but slow, in his performances. Shakespeare, with the English man-of-war, lesser in bulk, but lighter in sailing, could turn with all tides, tack about, and take advantage of all winds, by the quickness of his wit and invention."

Among the actors who, with Shakespeare, took part in the first production of Jonson's *Every Man in His Humour* was Christopher Beeston, who when he died in 1637 was manager of the Cockpit Theater in Drury Lane. He was succeeded in this office by his son William, who became in his old age the revered transmitter to Restoration players and playwrights of the traditions of the great age in which he had spent his youth. From him, and from another actor of the same period, John Lacy, as well as from other sources, the antiquary John Aubrey collected fragments of gossip for his lives of the English poets. According to Aubrey's notes, confused and unequal in value, Shakespeare "did act exceeding well"; "understood Latin pretty well, for he had been in his younger years a schoolmaster in the country"; "was a handsome, well-shaped man, very good company, and of a very ready and pleasant smooth wit." It is Aubrey, too, that reports that John Shakespeare was a butcher, and he adds, "I have been told heretofore by some of the neighbours that when he was a boy he exercised his father's trade. . . . When he killed a calf, he would doe it in a high style and make a speech. There was at that time another butcher's son in this towne, that was held not at all inferior to him for a naturall wit, his acquaintance, and coetanean, but dyed young." The same writer is authority for the statement that it was at Grendon, near Oxford, on the road from Stratford to London, that the dramatist "happened to take the humour of the constable in Midsummer Night's Dream" — a remark that may refer loosely either to Bottom and his friends, or to Dogberry or to Dull. He also ascribes to the poet an apocryphal epigram on a Stratford usurer, John Combe.

The Rev. John Ward, vicar of Stratford-on-Avon from 1662 to 1668, kept about the time of his coming to this charge a diary in which he relates certain echoes of the conversation of the town at a time when the poet's nephews were still living there. From him we hear that in his elder days Shakespeare retired to Stratford; that in his most active period he wrote two plays a year; that he spent at the rate of £1000 a year; and that his death was due to a fever following a "merry meeting" in Stratford with Jonson and Drayton.

An additional reference to the tradition of Shakespeare's convivial tendencies is to be found in the legend of his visit to Bidford, six miles from Stratford,

with a group of cronies to compare capacities with the
Bidford Drinkers. According to the earliest version
of this somewhat widespread tale, that of a visitor
to Stratford in 1762, "he enquired of a shepherd for
the Bidford Drinkers, who replied they were absent
but the Bidford sippers were at home, and, I suppose,
continued the sheepkeeper, they will be sufficient for
you; and so, indeed, they were; he was forced to take
up his lodging under that tree [the crab-tree, long
pointed out] for some hours."

The following reference to Shakespeare's father is
found in the memoranda of Archdeacon Plume of
Rochester, written about 1656. "Sir John Mennes
saw once his old father in his shop — a merry cheeked
old man that said, 'Will was a good honest fellow,
but he darest have crackt a jest with him at any
time.'" No Sir John Mennes who could have seen
John Shakespeare is known, but the saying may well
be the echo of contemporary gossip.

A manuscript preserved at Corpus Christi College,
Oxford, contains certains notes made before 1688 by the
Rev. William Fulman. Among them are interpolated
others (given here in italics) by the Rev. Richard
Davies previously to 1708. "William Shakespeare was
born at Stratford-on-Avon in Warwickshire about
1563–4. *Much given to all unluckinesse in stealing
venison and rabbits, particularly from Sr. . . . Lucy, who
had him whipt and sometimes imprisoned, and at last
made him fly his native country to his great advancement;*

*but his reveng was so sweet that he is his Justice Clodpate,
and calls him a great man, and that in allusion to his
name bore three lowses rampant for his arms.* From an
actor of playes he became a composer. He dyed Apr.
23, 1616, ætat 53, probably at Stratford, for there he
is buried, and hath a monument (Dugd. p. 520), *on
which he lays a heavy curse upon any one who shall
remove his bones. He dyed a papist.*" The inaccuracy
of Davies's version of facts otherwise known warns
us against too great a reliance on his individual contribution.

A certain John Dowdall left a short account of places
he visited in Warwickshire in 1693. He describes the
monument and tombstone, giving inscriptions, and
adds, "The clarke that shew'd me this church is
above 80 years old; he says that this Shakespeare was
formerly in this towne bound apprentice to a butcher,
but that he run from his master to London, and there
was received into the play-house as a serviture, and by
this means had an opportunity to be what he afterwards prov'd. He was the best of his family, but the
male line is extinguished. Not one for feare of the curse
abovesaid dare touch his gravestone, tho his wife and
daughters did earnestly desire to be leyd in the same
grave with him." The traditional explanation of the
curse as reported by William Hall, has already been
given (p. 35).

The first regular biography of Shakespeare is that
by Nicholas Rowe, written as a preface to his edition of

the plays which, issued in 1709, stands at the beginning
of modern Shakespearean interpretation. Though
compiled nearly a century after the poet's death,
Rowe's life has claims upon our credit more substantial
than might be expected. His chief source of information was the great actor Betterton, a Shakespeare
enthusiast, who had himself taken pains to accumulate
facts concerning his hero. Much of Betterton's
material came to him through John Lowin and Joseph
Taylor, two actors who had been colleagues of Shakespeare's and who lived into the Restoration period.
According to John Downes, a theatrical prompter at
the end of the seventeenth century, these veterans
brought to the new generation the actual instruction
they had received from the dramatist himself on the
playing of the parts respectively of Henry VIII and
Hamlet. Theatrical and other traditions reached
Rowe also through Sir William D'Avenant, the leading
figure in the revival of the stage after 1660. D'Avenant's father was host of the Crown Inn at Oxford,
where, according to the statements of Aubrey and
of Anthony Wood in 1692, Shakespeare was accustomed
to put up on his journeys between London and Stratford. Wood reports that the elder D'Avenant was a
"man of grave and saturnine disposition, yet an admirer
of plays and play-makers, especially Shakespeare,"
and that Mrs. D'Avenant was "a very beautiful
woman, of a good wit and conversation." William
D'Avenant was generally reputed to be Shakespeare's

godson, and Aubrey, whose gossip must be accepted
with great hesitation, says that he was not averse
to being taken as his son.   In spite of the fact of this
scandal's appearance in various seventeenth century
anecdotes, the more careful account of the D'Avenants
by Wood points to its rejection.   The story is usually
linked with another recorded by the lawyer Manningham in his Diary, March 13, 1602, that Burbage, who
had been playing Richard III, was overheard by Shakespeare making an appointment with a lady in the
audience.   When the tragedian arrived at the rendez-
vous, he found Shakespeare in possession; and on
knocking was answered that "William the Conqueror
was before Richard the Third."

To return to the D'Avenants, the elder son, Robert,
used to tell that when he was a child Shakespeare had
given him "a hundred kisses."   Sir William was
Rowe's authority for the statement that the Earl of
Southampton once gave the poet £1000 "to enable
him to go through with a purchase which he heard he
had a mind to"; but no purchase of this magnitude by
Shakespeare is recorded.   D'Avenant himself was said
to own a complimentary letter written to Shakespeare
by James I, and the publisher Lintot says that the
Duke of Buckinghamshire claimed to have examined
the document.   The story about Shakespeare's first
connection with the theater consisting in his holding
horses outside, told first in a manuscript note preserved
in the Library of the University of Edinburgh, 1748,

is also credited to D'Avenant. According to this tradition, frequently repeated, the future dramatist organized a regular corps of boys and monopolized the business, so that "as long as the practice of riding to the play-house continued the waiters that held the horses retained the appellation of Shakespeare's Boys."

Many of the natural inferences to be drawn from the data in the first part of the chapter are given by Rowe as facts. Thus he states positively that Shakespeare attended a free school, from which he was withdrawn owing to "the narrowness of his circumstances, and the want of assistance at home." He repeats the deer-stealing anecdote, with further detail. As to his acting, Rowe reports, "Tho' I have inquir'd, I could never meet with any further account of him this way than that the top of his performance was the ghost in his own Hamlet." He corroborates the general contemporary opinion of Shakespeare's fluency and spontaneity in composition. As to his personality, he says, "Besides the advantages of his wit, he was in himself a good-natur'd man, of great sweetness in his manners and a most agreeable companion." Rowe credits Shakespeare with having prevented his company from rejecting one of Jonson's plays at a time when Jonson was altogether unknown, and is inclined to consider the latter ungenerous in his critical remarks on Shakespeare.

William Oldys, in his manuscript *Adversaria*, now in the British Museum, reports a few further fragments of gossip, the chief of which is that Shakespeare's brother Gilbert was discovered still living about 1660 and was questioned by some actors as to his memory of William. All he could give them was a vague recollection of his having played the part of Adam in *As You Like It*.

Such are the most significant details which tradition, unauthenticated but often plausible, has added to our knowledge of the documents. There exists also a very considerable amount of literary allusion to Shakespeare's productions from 1594 onwards, which is easily accessible in collected form. The most notable of these are the comments of his friend and contemporary, Ben Jonson. Besides the splendid eulogy prefixed to the First Folio, Jonson talked of Shakespeare's lack of art to Drummond of Hawthornden, and expressed himself with affection and discrimination in the famous passage in *Timber*.

After all allowances have been made for the inaccuracies of oral tradition, we may safely gather from those concerning Shakespeare some inferences which help to clothe the naked skeleton of the documented facts. It is clear that, within a generation after Shakespeare's death, common opinion both in Stratford and London recognized that in the actor and dramatist a great man had passed away, that he had been in a worldly sense highly successful, though starting from unpropitious beginnings, that he wrote with great swiftness and ease, and that in his personal relations he was gentle, kindly, genial, and witty. That the

bailiff's son who returned to his native town as a prosperous gentleman, is to be identified with the actor and
shareholder of the London theaters, and with the
author of the plays and poems, it is difficult to see
how there can remain any reasonable doubt; and,
though the facts which prove this identity contain little
to illuminate the vast intellect and soaring imagination
which created Hamlet and Lear, they contain nothing
irreconcilable with the personality which these creations
imply rather than reveal.

One further source of information about Shakespeare's personality has figured largely in some biog-
raphies. The *Sonnets* were published in 1609, evi-
dently without Shakespeare's coöperation or consent,
with a dedication by the publisher, Thomas Thorpe, to
a Mr. W. H., " the onlie begetter of these insuing
sonnets." All attempts to identify this Mr. W. H.
have failed. He may have been merely the person who
procured the manuscript for Thorpe, though the
language of the dedication seems to imply that he was
the young gentleman who is the subject of a considerable number of the poems. Of this young gentleman
and of a dark lady who seems to have been the occasion
of other of the sonnets, much has been written, but no
facts of Shakespeare's life have been established beyond
those which are obvious to every reader : that Shakespeare wrote admiring and flattering sonnets to a young
man who is urged to marry (and who may have been
the Earl of Southampton, or an unknown Mr. W. H.,

or another); and that he treats of an intrigue with some unknown woman. The identification of the young man of the first seventeen sonnets with other friends who are praised in later sonnets is not certain, though in some cases probable; and much research and conjecture have entirely failed to make clear the relations between the poet, the rival poet, the lady, and the friend. The *Sonnets* furnish us with no knowledge of Shakespeare's personal affairs, and only a meager basis even for gossip as to some of his experiences with men and women.

Another kind of inquiry has sought to discover in the sonnets not facts or incidents of Shakespeare's life, but indications of his emotional experiences. The results of such inquiry are manifestly outside the scope of this chapter. For their discussion, the reader must be referred to Professor Alden's comprehensive Variorum edition of the *Sonnets*. Shakespeare's personality as it is reflected from his works will also be considered in the concluding chapter of this volume. So much stress, however, has been placed on interpretations of the sonnets, and these have so often occupied an exaggerated place in his biography, that it may be worth while to remark that, whether these lyrical poems are genuine and personal or are conventional and literary, and whether they make the poet more clearly discernible or not, they must certainly be taken not alone by themselves, but in connection with the dramas as affording us an impression of the man who wrote them.

Of the sonnets, it may be said in almost the same words just now used of the documents and traditions, that whether they contain much or little to illuminate the vast intellect and soaring imagination which created Hamlet and Lear, they contain nothing irreconcilable with the personality which these creations imply rather than reveal.

There are, scattered throughout the plays, a few unmistakable allusions to contemporary events, but they do not go far as indications of Shakespeare's political attitude. Such passages as the references to Queen Elizabeth in *Midsummer-Night's Dream*, to King James and the King's Evil in *Macbeth*, or to the return of Essex from Ireland in *Henry V*, are in harmony with the popular feeling of the time, and show no individual traits. Attempts to read a play like *Hamlet* as a political allegory are ingenious but unconvincing. The treatment of the mob in several plays has been thought to prove Shakespeare undemocratic, but the weakness of aristocratic arrogance in *Coriolanus* is just as impressive. Critics have found reasons for thinking him a Catholic, an Anglican, a Puritan, a free-thinker; but the conflict of their opinions only shows how well the dramatist kept his secret.

> Others abide our question. Thou art free.
> We ask and ask — Thou smilest and art still,
> Out-topping knowledge.

CHAPTER III

SHAKESPEARE'S READING

WE have called the present chapter "Shakespeare's Reading" rather than "The Learning of Shakespeare," because, apart from the famous line in which Ben Jonson stated that the poet had "small Latin and less Greek," it is evident from the allusions throughout the plays that Shakespeare was a reader rather than a scholar. In other words, he used books for what interested him; he did not study them for complete mastery; and many and varied as are the traces of his literary interests, they have the air of being detached fragments that have stuck in a plastic and retentive mind, not pieces of systematic erudition. It is true that many books have been written to show that Shakespeare had the knowledge of a professional in law, medicine, navigation, theology, conveyancing, hunting and hawking, horsemanship, politics, and other fields; but such works are usually the products of enthusiasts in single subjects, who are apt to forget how much a man of acute mind and keen observation can pick up of a technical matter that interests him for the time, and how intelligently he can use it. The cross-examination of an expert witness by an able lawyer is an everyday illustration; and in the literature of our own day this kind of versatility is strikingly exemplified in the work of such a writer as Mr. Kipling.

How Shakespeare learned to read and write his own tongue we do not know; that he did learn hardly needs to be argued. The free grammar school at Stratford-on-Avon, like other schools of its type, was named from its function of teaching Latin grammar; and we may make what is known of the curricula of such schools in the sixteenth century the basis for our inferences as to what Shakespeare learned there.

The accidence, with which the course began, was studied in Lily's Grammar, and clear echoes of this well-known work are heard in the conversation between Sir Hugh Evans and William Page in *The Merry Wives of Windsor*, IV. i, in *1 Henry IV*, II. i. 104, in *Much Ado*, IV. i. 22, in *Love's Labour's Lost*, IV. ii. 82 (and perhaps, V. i. 10 and 84), in *Twelfth Night*, II. iii. 2, in *The Taming of the Shrew*, I. i. 167, — a line of Terence altered by Lily, — and in *Titus Andronicus*, IV. ii. 20–23, where Demetrius reads two lines from Horace, and Chiron says,

> O, 'tis a verse in Horace; I know it well.
> I read it in the grammar long ago.

Such fragments of Latin as we find in the dialogue between Holofernes and Nathaniel in *Love's Labour's Lost*, IV. ii, and V. i, are probably due to some elementary phrase-book no longer to be identified. It is to be noted how prominently this early comedy figures in the list of evidences of his school-day memories.

Among the first pieces of connected Latin prose read in the Elizabethan schools was *Æsop's Fables*, a collection which, after centuries of rewriting and recompiling for adults, had come in the sixteenth century to be regarded chiefly as a school-book, but allusions to which are everywhere to be found in the literature of the day. In *2 Henry VI*, III. i. 343, and *Richard II*, III. ii. 129, we find references to the fable of "The Countryman and a Snake"; in *2 Henry VI*, III. i. 69, and *Timon of Athens*, II. i. 28, to "The Crow in Borrowed Feathers"; in *2 Henry VI*, III. i. 77, to "The Wolf in the Sheep's Skin"; in *King John*, II. i. 139, to "The Ass in the Lion's Skin"; in *Henry V*, IV. iii. 91, to "The Hunter and the Bear"; in *As You Like It*, I. i. 87, to "The Dog that Lost his Teeth"; in *All's Well*, II. i. 71, to "The Fox and the Grapes"; besides a number of slighter and less definite allusions. The most detailed fable in Shakespeare, that of "The Belly and the Members," in *Coriolanus*, I. i. 99, is derived, not from *Æsop*, but from Plutarch's *Life of Coriolanus*.

The traces of the well-known collection of sayings from various writers called *Sententiæ Pueriles*, and of the so-called *Distichs of Cato*, both of which were commonly read in the second and third years, are only slight. Battista Spagnuoli Mantuanus, whose *Eclogues*, written about 1500, had become a text-book, is honored with explicit mention as well as quotation in *Love's Labour's Lost*, IV. ii. 95. Cicero, who was read from

the fourth year, has left his mark on only a phrase or
two, in spite of his importance in Renaissance culture;
but Ovid is much more important. The motto on
the title-page of *Venus and Adonis* is from the *Amores*,
and the matter of the poem is from *Metamorphoses*, X.
519 ff., with features from the stories of Hermaphroditus
and Salmacis (*Meta.* IV. 285 ff.), and the hunting in
Calydon (*Meta.* VIII. 270 ff.). Ovid is quoted in Latin
in three early plays; and even where a translation
was available, the phrasing of Shakespeare's allusions
sometimes shows knowledge of the original. Most of
Ovid had been translated into English before Shakespeare began to write, and Golding's version of the
Metamorphoses (1567) was used for the references to
the Actæon myth in *A Midsummer-Night's Dream*,
IV. i. 107 ff., and for a famous passage in *The Tempest*,
V. i. 33. Livy, who had been translated in 1545
according to Malone, seems to have been the chief
source of *Lucrece*, with some aid from Ovid's *Fasti*, II.
721 ff. Among other Ovidian allusions are those to
the story of Philomela, so pervasive in *Titus Andronicus;* to the Medea myth in four or five passages; to
Narcissus and Echo, Phaeton, Niobe, Hercules, and a
score more of the familiar names of classical mythology.
Pyramus and Thisbe Shakespeare may have read about
in Chaucer as well as in Ovid, but Bottom's treatment
of this story in *A Midsummer-Night's Dream* gives but
a slight basis for proving literary relations.

Virgil followed Ovid in the fifth year, and with Virgil,

Terence. Of direct knowledge of the latter the plays bear no trace, but of the former there seems to be an influence in the description of the painting of Troy in *Lucrece*, 1366 ff., and in two short Latin sentences in *2 Henry VI*, II. i. 24, and IV. i. 117. Horace, Plautus, Juvenal, Persius, and Seneca were the new authors taken up in the last years in school. All the Horace in the plays may have been taken from other works, like the passage already quoted from Lily's Grammar. Juvenal and Persius have left no mark. The *Menæchmi* and *Amphitruo* of Plautus furnish the basis for *The Comedy of Errors*, and no English translation of either of these is known before that of the *Menæchmi* in 1595, which some critics think Shakespeare may have seen in manuscript. But no verbal similarities confirm this conjecture, and there is no reason why the dramatist should not have known both plays at first hand.

The influence of Seneca is dramatically the most important among the classical authors. All the plays that go by his name had been translated into English in the first part of Elizabeth's reign; he was the main channel through which the forms of classical tragedy reached the Renaissance; and when Shakespeare began to write he was the dominant force in the field of tragedy. This makes it hard to say whether the Senecan features in *Titus Andronicus*, *Richard III*, and even *Hamlet*, are due to Seneca directly, or to the tradition already well established among Shakespeare's earlier contemporaries.

The impression which the evidence from the text-
books as a whole leaves on one is that Shakespeare
took from school enough Latin to handle an occasional
quotation [1] and to extract the plot of a play, but that
he probably preferred to use a translation when one
was to be had. The slight acquaintance shown with
authors not always read at school, Caesar, Livy, Lucan,
and Pliny, does not materially alter this impression.
Much more conclusive as to the effect of his Latin
training than the literary allusions are the numerous
words of Latin origin either coined by Shakespeare, or
used in such a way as to imply a knowledge of their
derivation. The discovery of a lost translation may
modify our views as to whether a particular author
was used by him in the original, but the evidence from
his use of Romance words gives clear proof that his
schooling was no unimportant element in his mastery
of speech.

Greek was occasionally begun in the Elizabethan
grammar school, but we do not know whether this
was the case in Stratford. Certainly we have no
reason to believe that Shakespeare could read Greek,
as all his knowledge of Greek authors could have been
obtained from translations, and only two Greek words,
misanthropos and *threnos*, occur in his writings. Yet
no single author was so important in providing material
for the plays as the Greek Plutarch. His *Lives of
Julius Cæsar, Marcus Brutus, Marcus Antonius,* and

[1] See the list in the appendix to Schmidt's *Lexicon.*

Caius Martius Coriolanus, in Sir Thomas North's translation, are the direct sources of the great Roman tragedies, and in a less important way the *Lives of Antonius* and *Alcibiades* were used in *Timon of Athens*. Homeric elements are discoverable in *Troilus and Cressida*, which derives mainly from the medieval tradition. As the Trojan story was already familiar on the stage, these need not have come from Chapman's Homer. The knowledge of Lucian which seems implied in *Timon* was probably not gained from the Greek original. The late Greek romances, which were popular in translation, may have been read by Shakespeare, since the reference to the "Egyptian thief" in *Twelfth Night*, V. i. 120, is from the *Æthiopica* of Heliodorus, translated in 1569. Attempts have been made by the assembling of parallel passages to prove a knowledge of Greek tragedy on the part of Shakespeare, but such parallelisms are more naturally explained as coincidences arising from the treatment of analogous themes and situations.

Of modern languages, French was the easiest for an Elizabethan Englishman to acquire, and the French passages and scenes in *Henry V* make it fairly certain that Shakespeare had a working knowledge of this tongue. Yet, as in the case of Latin, he seems to have preferred a translation to an original when he could find it. Montaigne, whose influence some have found pervasive in Shakespeare, he certainly used in Gonzalo's account of his ideal commonwealth in *The*

Tempest, II. i. 143 ff., but it seems that he employed
Florio's translation here. Rabelais's Gargantua is
explicitly mentioned in *As You Like It,* III, ii. 238,
and the great humorist is possibly the inspirer of
some of Sir Andrew's nonsense in *Twelfth Night,* II. iii.
23. Many of the Sonnets contain reminiscences of
the French sonneteers of the sixteenth century, and
it is thought that in some cases Shakespeare shows
direct acquaintance with Ronsard. He was thus acquainted with the three greatest French writers of
his century, and French may well have been the
medium through which he reached authors in other
languages.

The class of Italian literature with which Shakespeare shows most acquaintance is that of the *novelle,*
though there is no proof that he could read the language. The *Decameron* of Boccaccio contains the love-
story of *Cymbeline,* though there may have been an
intermediary; the plot of *All's Well* came from the
same collection, but had been translated by Painter in
his *Palace of Pleasure;* and the story of the caskets
in *The Merchant of Venice* is found in a form closer to
Shakespeare's in the English translation of the *Gesta
Romanorum* than in the *Decameron.* Thus we cannot
conclude that the poet knew this work as a whole.
Similarly with Bandello and Cinthio. The plot of
Much Ado is found in the former, and is translated by
Belleforest into French, but at least one detail seems
to come from Ariosto, and here again an intermediary

is commonly conjectured. The novel from Cinthio's *Hecatommithi* which formed the basis of *Othello* existed in a French translation; and his form of the plot of *Measure for Measure* came to Shakespeare through the English dramatic version of George Whetstone. The version of the bond story in *The Merchant of Venice* closest to the play is in *Il Pecorone* of Sir Giovanni Fiorentino, but the tale is widespread. Incidents in *The Merry Wives* have sources or parallels in the same work, in Straparola's *Piacevoli Notti*, and in Bandello, but in both cases English versions were available. A mass of Italian and French prototypes lies behind the plot of *Twelfth Night*, but most of the details are to be found in the English *Apolonius and Silla* of Barnabe Riche, and there is reason to conjecture a lost English play on the subject. *The Taming of the Shrew*, based on an extant older play, draws also on Gascoigne's version of Ariosto's *I Suppositi;* and the echoes of Petrarch in the Sonnets may well have come through French and English imitators. The introduction of stock types from the Italian drama, such as the pedant and the braggart-soldier, can be accounted for by the previous knowledge of these in England, and does not imply a first-hand reading of Italian literature. The negative position is still stronger in the case of Spanish, where the use of episodes from George of Montemayor's *Diana* in *The Two Gentlemen*, *Twelfth Night*, and *A Midsummer-Night's Dream*, can be supposed to be due to the author's having access to Yonge's translation in manuscript, especially since there is no other trace of Spanish influence.

The conclusion with regard to Italian and Spanish, then, seems to be that Shakespeare in his search for plots was aware of the riches of the *novelle*, but that he found what he wanted as a rule in English or French versions; and that we have no evidence of his knowledge of anything but fiction from these literatures.

Turning now to English, we find Shakespeare's knowledge of books in his own tongue beginning after the Conquest. The romances of the Middle Ages were in the Elizabethan time rapidly undergoing the process of degradation that was soon to end in the chap-books, but the material was still widely known. The particular versions read by the dramatist can rarely be determined on account of the slight nature of most of the references, but we find allusions to the Arthurian romances, to *Guy of Warwick*, *Bevis of Hampton*, *The Squire of Low Degree*, Roland and Oliver, and to *Huon of Bordeaux*, from which last came the name of Oberon as king of the fairies. Among popular ballads, those of Robin Hood are frequently alluded to; the story of *King Cophetua and the Beggar Maid* appears in no fewer than five plays; Hamlet knew a ballad on Jephtha's daughter, and Sir Toby one on the chaste Susanna. A large number of popular songs appear in fragments; and rimes and spells, current jests and anecdotes, combine with the fairy-lore of *A Midsummer-Night's Dream,*

Romeo and Juliet, and *The Merry Wives* to assure us
that Shakespeare was thoroughly versed in the literature and traditions of the people.

His acquaintance with more formal letters begins
with Chaucer, whose *Knight's Tale* contributed some
details to *A Midsummer-Night's Dream*, and the main
plot of *The Two Noble Kinsmen*, in which Shakespeare is
now usually supposed to have had a hand. This story
had, however, been already dramatized by Richard
Edwardes. More certainly direct is his knowledge of
Chaucer's *Troilus*, which, with Caxton's *Recuyell of
the Historyes of Troye*, is the main source of *Troilus
and Cressida*. The references to the leprosy of Cressida
are due to Henryson's *Testament of Creseide*, a Scots
sequel to Chaucer's poem, printed in the sixteenth century editions of the older poet's works. In the *Legend
of Good Women* he may have found the story of Pyramus,
and a version of the tragedy of Lucrece, to supplement
his main sources in Livy and Ovid Chaucer's contemporary Gower contributed to his stock the story of
Florent (*Taming of the Shrew*, I. ii. 69) from the *Confessio
Amantis*, and from the same collection a version of the
tale of *Apollonius of Tyre*, dramatized by Shakespeare
and another in *Pericles*.

With the non-dramatic literature produced by Shakespeare's contemporaries, we naturally find most evidence
of his acquaintance in the case of those books which
provided material for his plays. Thus the otherwise
obscure Arthur Brooke, whose poem *Romeus and Juliet*

is the chief source of the tragedy, is much more prominent in such an enumeration as the present than he
probably was in Shakespeare's view of the literature
of the day. Painter, whose version of the same story
in his *Palace of Pleasure* cannot be shown to have been
used much, if at all, by the dramatist, seems nevertheless to have been known to him; and we hardly need
evidence that Shakespeare must have kept a watchful
eye on similar collections of stories, such as Whetstone's,
Riche's, and Pettie's. Of the greater writers of imaginative literature there is none missing from the list of
those he knew, though, as has been implied, the evidence is not always proportionate to the greatness;
and some prominent figures in other fields, such as
Hooker and Bacon, do not appear. Spenser, who is
supposed to have alluded to Shakespeare in *Colin Clout's
come home again* and, less probably, in *The Teares of
the Muses*, is in turn alluded to in *A Midsummer-Night's
Dream*, V. i. 52; and his version of the story of Lear in
The Faerie Queene, II. x, is believed to have given Shakespeare his form of the name Cordelia. Evidence is more
abundant in the case of Sir Philip Sidney. The under-
plot of *King Lear* is based on the story of the blind king
of Paphlagonia in the *Arcadia*, and Sidney's sonnets,
along with those of Daniel, Drayton, Constable, Watson, and Barnes, formed the main channel through which
the French and Italian influences reached Shakespeare's.
However we may estimate the original element in his
sonnets, and in our opinion it is very great, there is no

question of the author's having had a thorough familiarity with contemporary sonnetteers.

Similarly we can be certain that he had read many of the elaborate narrative poems then in vogue, a class to which he contributed *Venus and Adonis*, *Lucrece*, and *A Lover's Complaint*. Daniel's *Rosamond* and Marlowe's *Hero and Leander* especially have left many traces, and Daniel's *Barons' Wars* is intimately related to *Richard II* and *Henry IV*. The longer prose fictions of the time he also watched, and Lyly's *Euphues* contributed the germ of a number of passages, as Lodge's *Rosalynde* and Greene's *Pandosto* supplied the plots of *As You Like It* and *The Winter's Tale* respectively.

Reference has already been made to his knowledge of folk beliefs about fairies. To this should be added other supernatural beliefs, especially as to ghosts, devils, and witches, evidence of his familiarity with which will occur to every one. Matters of this sort were much discussed in his time, the frequency of ghosts in Senecan plays having made them conspicuous in Elizabethan imitations, and religious controversy having stimulated interest in demonology. Several important books appeared on the subject, and one of these at least Shakespeare read, Harsnett's *Declaration of Egregious Popish Impostures*, for from it Edgar, as Poor Tom in *King Lear*, derived many of the names and phrases which occur in his pretended ravings.

The most useful book in all his reading, if we judge by the amount of his work that is based on it, was the second edition of the *Chronicles of England, Scotland, and Ireland*, compiled by Raphael Holinshed. With it he used the work by Hall on *The Union of Lancaster and York*, the *Chronicles* of Grafton and of Fabyan, and the *Annals* of John Stowe. On these were based the greater number of the historical plays, *Macbeth*, and the political part of *Cymbeline*. In the case of *Henry VIII* there should be added the *Acts and Monuments*, better known as the *Book of Martyrs*, of John Foxe.

To deal adequately with Shakespeare's reading in the plays of his time would be to write a history of the Elizabethan drama. Older dramatists, like Preston, Gascoigne, and Whetstone, he knew, for he quotes *Cambyses*, and from the two last he derives material for the plots of *The Taming of the Shrew* and *Measure for Measure*. Anonymous writers supplied the older plays on which he based *King John*, *King Lear*, and *Hamlet*, parts of *Henry V* and *VI*, and of *Richard III*, and probably others. Allusions prove a familiarity with all of Marlowe's dramas; *Hamlet* is indebted to the tradition of which Kyd was one of the founders; Lyly taught him much in the handling of light comic dialogue; and he quotes lines from Peele. Greene's contribution is less specifically marked; but Shakespeare's profession of acting, as well as that of play-writing, of necessity made him acquainted with the whole dramatic production of the time. Thus, as has been stated in a previous chapter, he acted in several of Jonson's plays, and a good case has been made out for his modelling his last comedies on the new successes of Beaumont and Fletcher.

No Englishman of that day was insensible to what was going on in exploration and conquest of the Western World; and in *The Tempest, Othello*, and other plays we have clear ground for stating that Shakespeare shared this interest, and read books like Eden's *History of Travayle in the West and East Indies*, Raleigh's *Discoverie of Guiana*, and such pamphlets as were used in the vast compilation of Richard Hakluyt. The scientific knowledge implied in the plays reflects current beliefs, and must have been derived from such works as Pliny, *Batman uppon Bartholome his Booke De Proprietatibus Rerum*, and from conversation.

Finally, Shakespeare knew his Bible. Several volumes have been written to exhibit the extent of this knowledge, and it has been shown by Anders that he knew both the Genevan and the Great Bible, as well as the Prayer Book.

Taken all together, the amount of literature indicated by this summary account of the evidences in the plays and poems abundantly proves the statement that Shakespeare, if not a scholar, was a man of wide and varied reading. When it is further considered that only a fraction of what any author reads leaves a mark that can be identified on what he writes, we shall readily allow that in the matter of study Shakespeare showed an activity and receptivity of mind that harmonizes with the impression received from his creative work.

It agrees with our impressions of him derived from other sources also, that his reading reflects not so much idiosyncrasies of taste as the prevalent literary interests of the day. Thus in Latin literature the most conspicuous author among general readers, as distinguished from scholars, was Ovid, whose romantic narratives appealed to a time which reveled in tales gathered from all quarters; and this same prominence of Ovid has been shown to exist among the classical authors known to the dramatist. Similarly his use of chronicles like that of Holinshed merely reflects a widespread interest in national history; and Shakespeare shared the popular interest in the translations of *novelle* and the like that poured in from the Continent. The age of Elizabeth was an age of great expansion in reading — especially in the literature of entertainment. For the first time since the introduction of printing the people were free to indulge in books as a recreation, and the enormous growth of publishing in this era indicates the response to the new demand. In all this Shakespeare took part, and the evidences appear in his works so far as the nature of their themes permitted it. But the drama gave no opportunity for anything but passing allusions to scientific, philosophical, and religious matters, so that direct evidence is lacking as to how far Shakespeare was acquainted with what was being written in these fields. On the other hand, the profundity of his insight into human motive and behavior, the evidences of prolonged and severe meditation on human life and the

F

ways of the world, and the richness of the philosophical generalizations that lie just below the surface of his greater plays, make it difficult to believe that in these fields also he did not join in the intellectual activity of his day.

CHAPTER IV

CHRONOLOGY AND DEVELOPMENT

THE value of a knowledge of the order in which an author's works were composed no longer needs to be argued. The development of power and skill which such knowledge reveals is an important part of biography, and an individual work is more surely interpreted when we know the period and the circumstances of the author's life in which it was written, and what other works, by himself and his fellows, lie nearest in point of time. Without a knowledge of chronology, the indebtedness of contemporary authors to one another and the growth of literary forms cannot be determined.

The fact, so often to be insisted upon, that at the beginning of Shakespeare's career stage plays were hardly regarded as literature at all and were not published by their authors, deprives us of the evidence usually afforded by date of publication. We are thus forced to have recourse to a variety of more or less casually recorded data, and to indications of differences of maturity in style and matter which are often much less clear than could be wished. Before giving the results of the research that has been pursued for a century and a half, it will be worth while to enumerate the most fruitful methods which have been employed, and the sorts of evidence available.

Of purely external evidence, the chief kinds are these : records of the performance of plays in letters, diaries, accounts, and the like; quotation, allusion, imitation, or parody in other works; entries in the books of the Master of the Revels at Court, and in the Register of the Stationers' Company; dates on the title-pages of the plays themselves; facts and traditions about the life of the author; dates in the lives of actors and in the careers of companies known to have performed the plays, and in the histories of theaters in which they were presented. Instances of some of these are the manuscript which tells of a performance of *The Comedy of Errors* at Gray's Inn in 1594; the diary of the quack, Dr. Simon Forman, who witnessed performances of *Macbeth*, *Cymbeline*, and *The Winter's Tale* at the Globe in 1610 and 1611; the appreciation of Shakespeare, with a list of a dozen plays by him, in the *Palladis Tamia* [1] of Francis Meres, 1598; and the pamphlets on Somers's voyage to Virginia, which offered suggestions for *The Tempest.*

Partly external and partly internal are the evidences derived from allusions in the plays to current events, personal or political, such as the reference in the Prologue to *Henry V* to the expedition of Essex to Ireland in 1599; references to other books, like the quotation from Marlowe in *As You Like It*, III. v. 82;

[1] See Appendix A, 13.

references from one play of Shakespeare's to another, like the promise in the Epilogue to *2 Henry IV* to "continue the story, with Sir John in it, and make you merry with fair Katherine of France."

The purely internal evidence is seldom as specific as the external, and requires to be handled with much judgment and caution. Most difficult in this class is the weighing of considerations of a moral or esthetic nature; for, though these are often powerful in their effect on the individual reader, they are usually incapable of proof to another person with different tastes and a different point of view. Of such tests, those afforded by a study of the methods used in the treatment of plot and in the development of character are perhaps the least subjective. Somewhat more palpable are the changing characteristics of style. The number and nature of classical allusions and Latin words and quotations; the kind and degree of elaboration of figures of speech, puns, conceits, and the like; diffuseness or concentration in the expression of thought; artificiality or lifelikeness in the treatment of dialogue; the use of prose or verse; the employment of oaths, checked by statute shortly after the accession of James I: these are the main aspects of style which can be used in determining, not exact dates, but the period of Shakespeare's activity within which a given work falls. More capable of mechanical calculation than the tests of either matter or style are those derived from changes in versification, though here too there is often a subjective element in the reckoning. The more important metrical tests include the following: the frequency of rhyme, whether in the heroic couplet or, as not uncommonly occurs in early plays, in alternates and even such elaborate arrangements as the sonnet; doggerel lines; alexandrines, or lines of twelve syllables; the presence of an extra syllable before a pause within the line; short lines, especially at the end of speeches; the substitution of other feet for the regular iambic movement of blank verse; weak and light endings; and, most valuable, the position of the pause in the line ("end-stopped" or "run on"), and feminine endings or hypermetrical lines, such as

" These many summers in a sea of glor-y."

Many of these variable features were not consciously manipulated by the author; and, even when a general drift in a certain direction is clearly observable in his practice with regard to them, it is not to be assumed that his progress was perfectly regular, without leaps forward and occasional returns to an earlier usage. It is to be noted also that the subject and atmosphere of a particular play might induce a metrical treatment of a special kind, in which case the verse tests would yield evidence not primarily chronological at all. Nevertheless, when all allowances have been made and all due caution exercised, it will be found that the indications of the versification corroborate and supplement the external evidences in a valuable way.

TABLE I

	Total No. of Lines	Prose	Blank Verse	Pentameter Rhymes	% Blank Verse w. Fem. Endings	% Run-on Lines	% Speeches Ending within the Line	No. of Light and Weak Endings
L. L. L. .	2785	1022	617	550	7.7	18.4	10.0	3
C. of E. .	1777	226	1156	216	16.6	12.9	0.6	0
T. G. of V. .	2292	659	1431	76	18.4	12.4	5.8	0
R. III F.₁ .	3589	63	3278	152	19.5	13.1	2.9	4
Q.₂	3456	63	3099	142	....	....	....	....
K. J. . .	2553	0	2403	128	6.3	17.7	12.7	7
R. & J. Q.₁	2156	259	1530	248	8.2	14.2	14.9	7
Q.₂	3051	455	2052	417	....	....	....	....
M. N. D. . .	2166	493	729	574	7.3	13.2	17.3	1
R. II . .	2756	0	2174	525	11.0	19.9	7.3	4
Merch. .	2656	604	1872	85	17.6	21.5	22.2	7
1 Hy. IV .	3176	1464	1561	80	5.1	22.8	14.2	7
2 Hy. IV .	3446	1857	1425	54	16.3	21.4	16.8	1
M.W. of W.Q.₁	1586	1303	148	34	....	....	....	
F.₁ .	3029	2703	207	65	27.2	20.1	20.5	1
Hy. V. .	3376	1367	1918	62	20.5	21.8	18.3	2
M. Ado .	2825	2106	618	18	22.9	19.3	20.7	2
J. C. . .	2477	156	2181	32	19.7	19.3	20.3	10
A. Y. L. I. .	2839	1679	871	58	25.5	17.1	21.6	2
T. N. . .	2690	1731	724	108	25.6	14.7	36.3	4
T. & C. .	3496	1188	2065	176	23.8	27.4	31.3	6
A. W. W. .	2966	1437	1176	251	29.4	28.4	74.0	13
Ham. Q.₁ .	2068	609	1155	54	....	....	....	....
Q.₂	3929	1200	2358	64	....	....	....	
F.₁ .	....	....	....	....	22.6	23.1	51.6	8
Meas. . .	2810	1134	1470	61	26.1	23.0	51.4	7
Oth. . .	3316	661	2549	78	28.1	19.5	41.4	2
Lear. . .	3328	952	2214	70	28.5	29.3	60.9	6
Mcb. . .	2108	158	1706	100	26.3	30.6	77.2	23
A. & C. .	3059	287	2589	34	26.5	43.3	77.5	99
Cor. . .	3406	829	2413	28	28.4	45.9	79.0	104
Cym. . .	3339	535	2528	90	30.7	46.0	85.0	130
W. T. . .	3074	979	1946	34	32.9	37.5	87.6	100
Temp. . .	2062	458	1390	4	35.4	41.5	84.5	87

TABLE II

COLLABORATED PLAYS

	TOTAL NO. OF LINES	PROSE	BLANK VERSE	PENTAMETER RHYMES	% BLANK VERSE W. FEM. ENDINGS	% RUN-ON LINES	% SPEECHES ENDING WITHIN THE LINE	NO. OF LIGHT AND WEAK ENDINGS
1 Hy. VI .	2677	0	2356	300	8.2	10.4	0.5	4
2 Hy. VI .	3162	492	2522	96	13.7	11.4	1.1	3
3 Hy. VI .	2914	0	2749	128	13.7	9.5	0.9	3
T. And. .	2523	43	2318	122	8.6	12.0	2.5	5
T. of Shr. .	2656	484	1948	94	17.7	8.1	3.6	14
T. of A. .	2361	660	1420	152	24.7	32.5	62.8	30 (S)
Per. . . .	2393	408	1341	268	20.2	18.2	71.0	82 (S)
Hy. VIII .	2759	179	2394	60	47.3	46.3	72.4	84 (S)
T. N. K. .	2822	160	2491	44	43.7	. . . . .	. . . .	. . . . .

The accompanying Tables[1] give the detailed results of investigations along these lines, and a study of the data therein contained will reveal both their possibilities and their limitations. In Tables I and II the order of the plays is approximately that of the dates of their composition (virtually the same as the dates of first performance). The second and third columns cannot be regarded as giving any clue to chronology, except that they show that in the dramas written under the influence of Marlowe prose is comparatively

[1] The figures here given are based in columns 1, 2, 3, and 4 on the calculations of Fleay ; in 5, 6, and 7 on those of König ; and in 8 on those of Ingram. (S) = Shakespeare's scenes.

rare. Elsewhere Shakespeare employed prose for a variety of purposes : for low comedy, as in the tavern scenes in *Henry IV*, and the scenes in which Sir Toby figures in *Twelfth Night;* for repartee, as in the wit-combats of Beatrice and Benedick; for purely intellectual and moralizing speeches, such as Hamlet's over the skull of Yorick. On the other hand, highly emotional scenes are usually in verse, as are romantic passages like the conversation of Lorenzo and Jessica in the moonlight at Belmont, or the dialogues of Fenton and Anne Page, which contrast with the realistic prose of the rest of the *Merry Wives* and also the artificial pastoralism of Silvius and Phœbe in *As You Like It.* Few absolute rules can be laid down in the matter, but study of Shakespeare's practice reveals an admirable tact in his choice of medium.

The frequency of rhyme, as shown in the fourth column, has more relation to date. While there is no very steady gradation, it is clear that in his earlier plays he used rhyme freely, while at the close of his career he had practically abandoned it. The large number of rhymes in *A Midsummer-Night's Dream* and *Romeo and Juliet* is accounted for mainly by the prevailing lyrical tone of a great part of these plays, while, on the other hand, in *All's Well* it probably points to survivals of an earlier first form of this comedy. It ought to be noted that, in the figures given here, the rhyming lines in the play scene in *Hamlet*, the vision in *Cymbeline*, the masque in *The Tempest*, and the Prologue and Epilogue of *Henry VIII* are not reckoned.

More significant are the percentages in columns five, six, and seven. Before 1598, feminine endings never reach twenty per cent of the total number of pentameter lines; after that date they are practically always above that number, and show a fairly steady increase to the thirty-five per cent of *The Tempest*. The variations of run-on lines (which, of course, carry with them the frequency of pauses within the line, and inversely the growing rarity of end-stopped lines) are closely parallel to those of the feminine endings; while the increase in the proportion of speeches ending within the line is still more striking. In *The Comedy of Errors* this phenomenon hardly occurs at all; in *The Tempest* it happens in over eighty-four per cent of the speeches, the increase being especially regular after 1598. Yet in some cases other causes are operative. Thus cuts and revisions of plays were apt to leave broken lines at the ends of speeches, and the comparatively high percentages in *Love's Labour's Lost*, *Romeo and Juliet*, and *All's Well* are probably in part due to these causes.

The phenomena recorded in the last column are peculiar. Previous to the date of *Macbeth* it appears that Shakespeare practically avoided ending a line with light or weak words such as prepositions, conjunctions, and auxiliary verbs, but that from about 1606 to the end he employed them in proportions ranging from 3.53 per cent in *Antony and Cleopatra* to 7.14 per cent in his part of *Henry VIII*.

The figures for plays not wholly written by Shakespeare are naturally less significant, and have therefore been given separately; yet, on the whole, they show the same general tendencies in the use of meter.

It will be observed that while the developments suggested by the different columns are fairly consistent, they do not absolutely agree in any two cases, and can obviously be used, as has been said, only to corroborate other evidence in placing a play in a period, not to fix a precise year. Further, in the calculations involved, there are many doubtful cases calling for the exercise of individual judgment, especially as to what constitutes a run-on line, or a light or weak ending. Thus Professor Bradley differs from König in several cases as to the figures given in the seventh column, counting the percentage of speeches ending within the line as 57 for *Hamlet*, 54 for *Othello*, 69 for *King Lear*, and 75 for *Macbeth*. For Acts III, IV, and V of *Pericles*, the 71 per cent is Bradley's, for which König's 17.1 is clearly a mistake. Serious as are such discrepancies, and suggestive of a need for a general re-counting of all the more significant phenomena, they are not so great as to shake the faith of any scholar who has seriously studied the matter in the usefulness of metrical tests as an aid in the settling of the chronology.

TABLE III

Periods	Comedies	Histories	Tragedies
I	L. L. L. 1591 C. of E. 1591 T. G. of V. 1591–2	1 Hy. VI 1590–1 2 Hy. VI 1590–2 3 Hy. VI 1590–2 R. III 1593 K. J. 1593	T. And. 1593–4
II	M. N. D. 1594–5 M. of V. 1595–6 T. of S. 1596–7 M. W. of W. 1598 M. Ado 1599 A. Y. L. I. 1599–1600 Tw. N. 1601	R. II 1595 1 Hy. IV 1597 2 Hy. IV 1598 Hy. V 1599	R. and J. 1594–5 J. Cæs. 1599
III	T. & C. 1601–2 A. Well 1602 Meas. 1603 Per. 1607–8		Ham. 1602, 1603 Oth. 1604 Lear 1605–6 Macb. 1606 T. of Ath. 1607 A. & Cl. 1607–8 Cor. 1609
IV	Cymb. 1610 W. Tale 1611 Temp. 1611 T. N. K. 1612–13	Hy. VIII 1612	

Table III gives a summary of the results of all the kinds of evidence available as recorded in the introduction to individual plays in the Tudor Shakespeare.   The

classification into Comedies, Histories, and Tragedies
draws attention at once to the changes in the type
of drama on which Shakespeare concentrated his
main attention, and suggests the usual division of
his activity into four periods. In the first of these,
extending from the beginning of his writing (perhaps
earlier than 1590) to the end of 1593, he attempted
practically all the forms of drama then in vogue.
Plays which were given him to revise, or in which he
was invited to collaborate, may naturally be supposed
to have preceded independent efforts, and his still
undetermined share in *Henry VI* is usually regarded
as his earliest dramatic production. What he learned
in this field of tragic history from his more experi-
enced fellows may be seen in *Richard III*, in which
he can be observed following in the footsteps of Marlowe
in the treatment of meter, in the rhetorical and lyrical
nature of the dialogue, and in the conception of the
central character. Even less of his individual quality
is to be discerned in the field of tragedy, for the most
that can be claimed for him in *Titus Andronicus* is
the re-combination of the repellent episodes of that
crude specimen of the tragedy of blood, and the re-
writing of the lines which occasionally cloak the horrors
with passages of poetry. If, as is unlikely, the first
form of *Romeo and Juliet* was written in this period,
the extant form must show it so radically revised that
it leaves us little ground for generalization as to his
power in tragedy in this first period.

It was in comedy that Shakespeare first showed originality. *Love's Labour's Lost* is one of the few plays whose plots seem to have been due to his own invention; and full of sparkle and grace as it is, it bears obvious marks of the *tour de force*, the young writer's conscious testing of his powers in social satire, in comic situation, and most of all in verbal mastery and the manipulation of dialogue. In *The Comedy of Errors* he had the advantage of a definite model in the well-defined type of the Plautian comedy; but here again in the doubling of the twins and the elaboration of the entanglements there are traces of the beginner's delight in technic for its own sake. The clearly contrasted types in the two pairs of heroes and heroines of *The Two Gentlemen of Verona* point to a conscious effort in characterization, as the author's attention had been concentrated on dialogue and on situation in the other two comedies of this group. Thus, regarding the variety of kind and the nature of his achievement in these first eight or nine plays, we can hardly fail to acquiesce in the general opinion that views the first period as one of experiment.

The chronicle history was the Elizabethan dramatic form whose possibilities were first exhausted. *King John* had been only a making over of an earlier work, and perhaps the most significant single change Shakespeare made was the excision of the anti-Romanist bias which in the older play had made John a Protestant hero. Yet this history voices, too, in the speeches of

Faulconbridge, that patriotic enthusiasm which finds fuller expression in the dying Gaunt's eulogy of England in *Richard II*, and culminates in the triumphant heroics of *Henry V*. This national enthusiasm, especially ebullient in the years following the Great Armada, is justly to be regarded as an important condition of the flourishing of these plays on English history; and it is natural to suppose that the ebbing of this spirit in the closing years of Elizabeth's reign is not unconnected with the decline of this dramatic type. There are, however, other causes clearly perceptible. The material was nearly exhausted. Almost every prominent national figure for the three hundred years before the founding of the Tudor dynasty had been put upon the stage; and to come down to more recent times was to meddle with matters of controversy, the ashes of which were not yet cold. The reign of Henry VIII was not touched till after the death of Elizabeth, and the nature of the treatment given to the court of her father by Shakespeare and Fletcher corroborates our view. Further, the growing mastery of technic which is so clearly perceptible in the comedies of the second period must have been accompanied by a restlessness under the hampering conditions as to the manipulation of character and plot which were imposed by the less plastic material of the chronicles. Some effort towards greater freedom the dramatist made in the later histories. The earlier plays of this class had been prevailingly tragic; but now he supplemented and enlivened the political element with the comic scenes which gave us Falstaff; yet these scenes, brilliant as they are in dialogue and superb in characterization, are of necessity little more than episodes. The form had served its purpose as an outlet for national feeling, but it was now outgrown. So distinguished, however, is Shakespeare's achievement in this kind that we might be almost justified in calling this second period that of the culmination of the chronicle history.

The main objection to this title lies in his contemporary accomplishment in comedy. *A Midsummer-Night's Dream* and *The Merchant of Venice*, the one in its graceful poetic fancy and dainty lyricism, the other in its balanced treatment of all the elements of dramatic effectiveness — action, character, and dialogue, — exhibit the dramatist in complete control of his technical instruments, the creator of masterpieces of romantic comedy. *The Taming of the Shrew* is a more or less perfunctory re-writing, possibly in collaboration, of an older farce comedy; *The Merry Wives of Windsor* bears on its face corroboration of the tradition that it was written to order in a fortnight. The power in high comedy first fully shown in *The Merchant of Venice* reaches its supreme pitch in the three plays composed at the turn of the century, *Much Ado about Nothing, As You Like It*, and *Twelfth Night*. In each of these a romantic love-tale, laid in some remote holiday world, is taken up, given a specific atmosphere, acted out by a group of delightful creations who are endowed with intellect, wit, and natural affection, bathed in poetic imagination, and yet handled with sufficient naturalism to awaken and hold our human sympathies. No more purely delightful form of dramatic art has ever been contrived; none has ever been treated so as to yield more fully its appropriate charm; so that in view of the completeness of the artist's success we are bound to call the period which closed with the first year of the seventeenth century the triumph of comedy.

Julius Cæsar, the first of the plays dealing with Roman history, may have been written before 1600, but, whether it preceded *Hamlet* by one year or three, it forms a gradual introduction to the group of the great tragedies. Masterly as it is in its delineation of types, rich in political wisdom and the knowledge of human nature, splendid in rhetoric, it still fails to rise to the intensity of passion that marks the succeeding dramas. In *Hamlet, Othello, King Lear*, and *Macbeth*, Shakespeare at length faced the great fundamental forces that operate in individual, family, and social life, realized especially those that make for moral and physical disaster, took account alike of the deepest tendencies in character and of the mystery of external fate or accident, exhibited these in action and reaction, in their simplicity and their complexity, and wrought out a series of spectacles of the pity and terror of human suffering and human sin without parallel in the modern

G

world. In these stupendous tragedies he availed himself of all the powers with which he was endowed and all the skill which he had acquired. His verse has liberated itself from the formalism and monotony that had marked it in the earlier plays, and is now free, varied, responsive to every mood and every type of passion; the language is laden almost to the breaking point with the weight of thought; the dialogue ranges from the lightest irony to heart-rending pathos and intolerable denunciation; the characters lose all semblance of artificial creations and challenge criticism and analysis like any personage in history; the action is pregnant with the profoundest significance. Hardly, if at all, less powerful are the later tragedies of the Roman group. *Antony and Cleopatra* is unsurpassed for the intensity of its picture of passion, for its superb mastery of language, for its relentless truth. The more somber scenes of *Coriolanus* convey a tragedy which either on its personal or its political side scarcely yields to its predecessors in poignancy and gloom. Whatever else he may have written in these years, here is surely the period of tragedy.

Nor do the plays classed as comedies and falling in the first three years of the new century seriously modify this impression of the prevailing tone of the period. *Troilus and Cressida*, *All's Well that Ends Well*, and *Measure for Measure* present a marked contrast to the romantic comedy of the preceding stage. The love-story of the first deals with a coquette and ends sordidly;

while in the political plot, though it gives occasion for
speeches full of weighty thinking, jealousy and intrigue
overwhelm the heroic element. The second, alone of
Shakespeare's comedies, has a hero who is a rake; and,
skilful as is the delineation of Helena, it needs all the
dramatist's power to hold our sympathy and to force
us to an unwilling assent to the title. *Measure for
Measure* has its scene laid in a city seething in moral
corruption: out of this rises the central situation of
the play; and the presence of the most idealistic of
Shakespeare's heroines does not avail to counter-
balance the atmosphere of sin and death that mocks
the conventional happy ending, and makes this play,
even more than the two others, seem more in place
among the tragedies than among the comedies.

The plays of the last period are, in the Folio, classed
with comedies, and such no doubt they are if judged
merely by the nature of their dénouements. But if
we consider their characteristic note, and the fact that
through the greater part of each play the forces and
passions involved are rather those operative in tragedy
than in comedy, we easily perceive why they have
been classed as tragi-comedies or dramatic romances.
Pericles in many respects stands apart from the other
three in nature as well as in date, for it is a dramatization of an old Greek romance, and in it the hand of
another than Shakespeare is only too evident. Yet
it shares with the others certain common features:
like *The Tempest* it has scenes at sea; all four deal with

the separation and reuniting of families; all show us sympathetic figures deeply wronged and finally over-coming their injurers by forgiveness. The abounding high spirits of the earlier comedies are here replaced by a mood of calm assurance of the ultimate triumph of good and a placid faith that survives a rude acquaint-ance with the evil that is in men's hearts. No period has a more distinctive quality than this of the dramatic romances, in which the dramatist, on the eve of his retirement from London, gave his imagination free play, and in both character and action stamped his last creations with the mark of a lofty idealism.

The obvious fitness of this fourfold division into periods inevitably raises the question of its causes, and attempts at an answer have run along two main lines. One of these has been followed out with much eloquence and persuasiveness by Professor Dowden, whose phrases "In the Workshop," "In the World," "In the Depths," "On the Heights," to describe the four periods, point clearly enough to the kind of significance which he finds in the changes in mood and type of play. With the first of these phrases few will be disposed to quarrel. In his period of experiment Shakespeare's style was as yet comparatively unformed, and his attention was so much occupied with problems of technic that even the most psychological of critics finds here little revelation of personality, and must be content to describe the stage as one of professional apprenticeship. In the terms used of the three later periods, however, there is an implication that the tone and mood of the plays in each are the direct reflection of the emotional experiences through which the poet himself was passing at the period of their composition. But this is to take for granted a theory of the relation between artist and production which has against it the general testimony of creator and critic alike. It is not at the pitch of an emotional experience that an artist successfully transmutes his life into art, but in retrospect, when his recollective imagination reproduces his mood in a form capable of being expressed without being dissipated. Of course, Shakespeare must have lived and enjoyed and suffered intensely; but this does not commit us to a belief in an immediate turning to account of personal experience in the writing of drama. His boy, Hamnet, died in 1596, about the time that he was writing *The Merchant of Venice* and the rollicking farce of *The Taming of the Shrew*, and just before he conceived Falstaff; it was fourteen years later that he gave us the pathetic figure of the young Mamillius in *The Winter's Tale*. From all we know of his personal life, the years of *King Lear* and *Othello* were years of abounding prosperity. The *lacrimæ rerum* that touch the mind in these stupendous tragedies are the outcome of profound meditation and vivid imagination, not the accompaniment of a cry of instant pain. However we are to reconstruct the spiritual biography of Shakespeare, it is clear that it is by no such simple reading of his life in terms of his treatment of comic or tragic themes.

The other line of explanation will suggest itself to any thoughtful student who contemplates the facts summed up in Chapter V on the Elizabethan drama. Whatever Shakespeare's preëminence in the quality of his work, he was not singular for innovations in kind. Not only are the plays of his experimental stage preceded by models easily discerned, but throughout his career one can see him eagerly taking up and developing varieties of drama on which less capable men had stumbled and for which the public had shown relish. Chronicle history, romantic comedy, tragedies of blood and revenge, dramatic romance, had all been invented by others, and Shakespeare never hesitated to follow their trail when it promised to lead to popular success. This does not mean that he did not put conscience into his work, but only that the change in type of play perceptible from period to period is more safely to be explained by changes of theatrical fashion and public taste than by conjectures as to the inner life of the dramatist. Nor are we prevented from finding here too that great good fortune as to occasion and opportunity that is needed, along with whatever natural endowment, to explain the achievement of Shakespeare. The return of the vogue of tragedy after he had attained maturity and seen life was indeed happy for him and for us; as was the rise of the imaginative type of dramatic romance when the storm and stress of his youth had gone by. Had the theatrical demand called for tragedy when Shakespeare was in the early thirties and light comedy when he was in the forties, it seems likely that he would have responded to the demand, though we can hardly suppose that the result would have been as fortunate as in the existing state of things it proved to be.

The foregoing discussion has been confined to Shakespeare's plays; the poems present problems of their own. *Venus and Adonis* (1593) and *Lucrece* (1594), indeed, resemble the plays of the first period, with which they are contemporary, both in conforming to a familiar type then much in vogue, the re-telling in ornate style of classical legends drawn chiefly from Ovid, and in exhibiting marks of the conscious exercise of technical dexterity. They show the Shakespeare of the dramas mainly in their revelation of a remarkable power of detailed observation and their richness of phrase and fluency of versification. Vivid and eloquent though they are, they can hardly be regarded as affording a sure prophecy of the passion and power of characterization that mark his mature dramatic production.

The case of the *Sonnets* is very different. From Meres's mention of them in 1598 we know that some had been written and were being circulated in manuscript by that date, and certain critics have sought to assign the main body of them to the first half of the last decade of the sixteenth century. But they were not published till 1609, and many of the greatest strike a note of emotion more profound than can be heard before the date of *Hamlet*. In writing them, Shakespeare was, to be sure, following a vogue, but as Professor Alden has pointed out in his introduction to them in the Tudor Shakespeare, they stand apart in important respects from the ordinary sonnet sequences of the time. All our researches have failed to tell us to whom they were addressed, if, indeed, they were addressed to any actual person at all; it is hardly necessary to urge that Shakespeare was capable of profound and passionate utterance under the impulse of imagination alone. The probability is that they were produced at intervals over a period of perhaps a dozen years, and that they represent a great variety of moods, impulses, and suggestions. While some of them betray signs of youth and remind us of the apprentice workman of *Love's Labour's Lost*, others display in their depth of thought, intensity of feeling, and superb power of incisive and concentrated expression, the full maturity of the man and the artist. Hardly in the great tragedies themselves is there clearer proof of Shakespeare's supremacy in thought and language.

CHAPTER V

The Elizabethan Drama

Shakespeare's lifetime was coincident with a period of extraordinary activity and achievement in the drama. By the date of his birth Europe was witnessing the passing of the religious drama that had held its course for some five centuries, and the creation of new and mixed forms under the incentive of classical tragedy and comedy These new forms were at first mainly written by scholars and performed by amateurs, but in England, as everywhere else in western Europe, the growth of a class of professional actors was threatening to make the drama popular, whether it should be new or old, classical or medieval, literary or farcical. Court, school, organizations of amateurs, and the strolling actors were all rivals in supplying a widespread desire for dramatic entertainment; and no boy who went to a grammar school could be ignorant that the drama was a form of literature which gave glory to Greece and Rome and might yet bestow its laurels on England.

When Shakespeare was twelve years old the first public playhouse was built in London. For a time literature held aloof from this public stage. Plays aiming at literary distinction were written for schools or court, or for the choir boys of St. Paul's and the royal chapel, who, however, gave plays in public as well as at court. But the professional companies prospered in their permanent theaters, and university men with literary ambitions were quick to turn to these theaters as offering a means of livelihood. By the time that Shakespeare was twenty-five, Lyly, Peele, and Greene had made comedies that were at once popular and literary; Kyd had written a tragedy that crowded the pit; and Marlowe had brought poetry and genius to triumph on the common stage — where they had played no part since the death of Euripides. A native literary drama had been created, its alliance with the public playhouses established, and at least some of its great traditions had been begun.

The development of the Elizabethan drama for the next twenty-five years is of exceptional interest to students of literary history, for in this brief period, in connection with the half-dozen theaters of a growing city and the demands of its varied population, we may trace the beginning, growth, florescence, and decay of many kinds of plays, and of many great careers. Actors, audiences, and dramatists all contributed to changes in taste and practice and to a development of unexampled rapidity and variety. In every detail of dramatic art there was change and improvement, a constant addition of new subject-matter, a mastery of new methods of technic, and an invention of new kinds of plays. The popular successes of Marlowe and Kyd

and the early plays of Shakespeare himself seemed old-
fashioned and crude to the taste of twenty years after,
yet the triumphs of Shakespeare's maturity failed to
exhaust the opportunities for innovation and advance.
We are amazed to-day at the mere number of plays
produced, as well as by the number of dramatists writing
at the same time for this London of two hundred thousand inhabitants. To realize how great was the
dramatic activity, we must remember further that
hosts of plays have been lost, and that probably there
is no author of note whose entire work has survived.
By the time, however, that Shakespeare withdrew
from London to Stratford the drama had reached its
height. The dozen years from 1600 to 1612 included
not only Shakespeare's great tragedies, but the best
plays of Jonson, Chapman, and Webster, and the
entire collaboration of Beaumont and Fletcher. The
only other decades comparable with this in the history
of the drama are that which heard plays by Sophocles,
Euripides, and Aristophanes and that other which saw
the masterpieces of Racine and Molière.

The greatness of the drama, however, by no means
ended with the retirement and death of Shakespeare.
Some of those who had been his early associates continued to write for the stage, and younger men, as
Fletcher, Massinger, Ford, and Shirley, carried on the
traditions of their predecessors. If, as in other forms
of literature, there was decline and decadence during
the next twenty-five years, the drama also retained

initiative, poetry, and intellectual force until the end.
It was not dead or dying when the outbreak of the Civil
War cut short its course; in fact, its plays, its traditions,
even some of its theaters, actors, and dramatists survived the suppression of twenty years and helped to
start the drama of the Restoration.   Had Shakespeare
lived to the age of seventy-eight he would have seen the
closing of the theaters, and his lifetime would have
covered the crowded history of the drama's development from such semi-moralities as *Cambises* and *The
Nice Wanton* to the last plays of Massinger and Shirley.

For nearly a quarter of a century he was a sharer in
this dramatic movement, working in London as actor,
manager, and playwright.   While no playwright was
more desirous than he to find in the stage full opportunity for his genius, he was as keen as any in gauging the
immediate theatrical demand and in meeting the varying conditions of a highly competitive profession.   As
we have already noted, he began by imitating those who
had won success, and to the end he was adroit in taking
advantage of a new dramatic fashion or discovery.
Like his fellows, he often took his plots from novels,
histories, or other narratives; but his very choice of
stories might be determined by the theatrical taste of
the moment, and in his treatment of those stories he
shows in person, situation, or scene, a consideration of
current practices, traditions, and conventions.   In
every field of literature, a writer is conditioned by the
work of his predecessors and contemporaries, and this

dependence on current taste is especially important in the drama, where practice tends to fix itself in convention, and where innovation to be successful requires coöperation from the actors and approval from the audience as well as genius from the author. Though Shakespeare is for all time, he is part and parcel of the Elizabethan drama. If his plays are Elizabethan in their defects and limitations, such as their trivial puns and word-play, their overcrowded imagery, their loose and broken structure, their paucity of female rôles, their mixture of comic and tragic, their reliance on disguise and mistaken identity as motives, their use of improbable or absurd stories; they are Elizabethan also in the qualities of their greatness, their variety of subject, their intense interest in the portrayal of character, the flexibility and audacity of their language, their noble and opulent verse, the exquisite idealism of their romantic love, and their profound analysis of the sources of human tragedy.

The Elizabethan drama was a continuation of the medieval drama transformed by the influence of classical models, especially the comedies of Terence and Plautus and the tragedies of Seneca. In England, by the beginning of the sixteenth century, the Miracle and Mystery plays were declining and were soon to disappear. The most common type of drama for the next sixty years was the Morality, which symbolized life as a conflict of vices and virtues or of the body and the soul. The drama was rapidly changing from long

out-door performances to brief plays that could be
given almost anywhere by a few actors. The term
Interludes became common for all such entertainments,
and allegorical frameworks served to contain a wide
variety of matter, farce, pedagogy, politics, religion,
history, or pageant. Close imitations of the classical
forms were soon attempted by scholars and men of
letters; but as the professional actors grew in importance the development of a national comedy and tragedy
went on without much direction from critics or theo-
rists, but rather in response to the demands of actors
and audiences and to the initiative of authors.

The developments of comedy were numerous. Allegory gradually disappeared, and the Morality ceased
to exist as a definite type, though its symbolization of
life and its concern with conduct were handed along to
the later drama. The plays of Robert Wilson, about
1580, show an interesting use of allegory for the purposes of social satire, and realism and satire long continued to characterize Elizabethan comedy, though for
a time confined mostly to incidental scenes. Common
and incidental also was farce, which is found in most
plays of the century whether tragic, comic, or moral
in their main purpose. Further, it was soon discovered
that the Plautian scheme of comedy was well suited to
farcical incident, as in *Gammer Gurton's Needle* (1552).[1]
The classical models or their Italian imitations also pro-

[1] In this chapter the dates appended to the plays indicate
the conjectured year of presentation. Dates of publication are
prefixed by *pr.*

duced other and less domestic imitations, as in Gascoigne's translation of Ariosto's *I Suppositi* (pr. 1566)
and Udall's *Ralph Roister Doister* (1540); a little later,
Lyly's *Mother Bombie*, Munday's *Two Italian Gentlemen*, and Shakespeare's *Comedy of Errors*. Indeed such
adaptations continued much later and resulted in some
of the best farces, or realistic comedies of intrigue, as
Shakespeare's *Merry Wives of Windsor* (1598), Heywood's *Wise Woman of Hogsdon* (1604), Jonson's
Epicene (1609) and *Alchemist* (1610).

The Plautian model, however, was far more influential than can be indicated by these close adaptations
or by any list of direct imitations or borrowings. For
the Elizabethan it offered a standard of comedy, and its
plots, persons, and devices were freely used in all kinds
of plays, romantic as well as realistic, sentimental as
well as satirical or farcical. The plots of Plautus and
Terence offer a series of tricks in which the complications are often increased by having the trickster tricked.
Certain fixed types of character play the parts of gulls
or gullers, as the old parents, the young lovers, the
parasite, the braggart soldier, and the clever slave.
The intrigue is forwarded by the use of disguise, mistaken identity, and most surprising coincidences; and
it is accomplished by dialogue, often gross and abusive,
but usually lively. This model served every nation
of western Europe, reappearing with prolonged vitality
in the inventions of Lope de Vega, the " commedia del
arte " of Italy, and in the masterpieces of Molière.

Much in its scheme that seems artificial and theatrical to-day was, we must remember, accepted without question by Europe of the sixteenth century as essential and desirable in comedy, especially in realistic comedy of intrigue or manners.

The plots of Terence, notably that of the *Andria*, also gave some encouragement to the modern fondness for adventure and sentimental love, and some classical sanction to the abundant romantic material that was knocking at the doors of comedy. If by romantic we mean what is strange and removed from ordinary experience and what has the attractions of wonder, thrill, and idealization, then for the Elizabethan the world of romance was a wide one. It included the medieval stories of knights and their gests, and also the fresher tales of classical mythology; the Americas and Indies of contemporary adventure and the artificial Arcadias of humanist imitators of Virgil and Theocritus. Ovid and Malory, Homer and Boccaccio, Drake and Sanazzaro, were all contributors. The union of this romance with comedy on the stage began in two ways, and principally under the innovation of two writers, Lyly and Greene.

The taste for pageants, processions, and tableaux grew and flourished under the patronage of the court; and music, dancing, and spectacle were combined with dialogue in various court exhibitions and plays given by the child actors. John Lyly, writing for these choir boys, developed this type of entertainment into a distinct species of comedy. Of his eight plays, written at intervals from 1580 to 1593, all but one were in prose, and all except the Plautian *Mother Bombie* adhere loosely to a common formula. Classical myth or story, with pastoral elements, and occasionally an allegory of contemporary politics, furnish the basis of plots with similar love complications. Gods, goddesses, nymphs, fairies, and many others add to the spectacle and mingle in the love intrigue, and all rise to a graceful dialogue, which quickens to brisk repartee when the pages or servants appear. The witty page supersedes the rude buffoon of earlier plays, and everything is graceful and ingenious, slight in serious interest, but relieved by movement and song.

This is the form of comedy which Shakespeare adopted for *Love's Labour's Lost* and perfected in *A Midsummer-Night's Dream*. But Lyly's contribution should not be defined merely by this type of drama, original as it is in its departure from medieval or classical precedents. He showed how comedy might be a courtly and literary entertainment and also the playground of fancy and wit.

The second development of romantic comedy came through the dramatization of stories of love, adventure, and marvels. To such stories Robert Greene gave a heightened charm through the idealization of his heroines. His *Friar Bacon and Friar Bungay* (1590) is a magic play with an historical setting; but the interest gathers and centers on the love story of Mar-

H

garet, the Keeper's daughter. In *James IV* (*c.* 1591) the pseudo-historical setting frames the stories of the noble Ida and the wronged but faithful Dorothea. In the incidents of the plot, with its woman disguised as a page, the faithless lover, and the final reconciliation, and also in the sweetness, modesty, and loyalty of the heroine, the play reminds us of Shakespeare's comedies and is indeed very close to *The Two Gentlemen of Verona*, in which he was clearly adopting Greene's formula.

Tragedy naturally lagged somewhat behind comedy as a form of popular entertainment. So far as we can judge from the extant plays, there was until the appearance of Kyd and Marlowe no real union between Senecan imitations like *Gorboduc* (1562), *Jocasta* (1566), and *The Misfortunes of Arthur* (1588), on the one hand, and popular medleys of morality, tragedy, and farce like *Cambises* (1565), *Horestes* (*pr.* 1567), and *Appius and Virginia* (1563), on the other. Marlowe's *Tamburlaine* (1587) was an epoch-making play because it brought to the popular drama true poetry and genuine passion; but it and its successors also established a new type of tragedy. Marlowe made no effort to retain the structure or themes of classical tragedy; on the contrary, he made his plays loosely connected series of scenes dealing with the life and death of the hero, crowded with persons and with startling action. In this he was conforming to the method of the dramatic narratives that pleased the theaters. But each play centers its dramatic interest on a mighty protagonist battling with his overweening desires and their inevitable disappointment. With the spectacle and sensation, the rant and absurdity, there is also dramatic structure and tragic significance in the revelation of these protagonists, their volitional struggles, and their direful catastrophes. These plays set the key for all Elizabethan tragedy, including Shakespeare's *Lear*, *Othello*, and *Macbeth*. They were immediately followed by dozens of imitators. All blank verse echoed Marlowe's mighty line, and tragedy was filled with ranting conquerors like Tamburlaine, monstrous villains like Barabbas, and murders like that of Edward II. Shakespeare was his pupil in the *2* and *3 Henry VI*, mastered his methods in *Richard III*, and still wrote in emulation, though no longer in imitation, in *Richard II* and *The Merchant of Venice*.

Within a few months of *Tamburlaine*, appeared a play of almost equal influence on subsequent drama, Kyd's *Spanish Tragedy*. Kyd was a student of Seneca, a translator of Garnier's *Cornelia*, a Senecan imitation; and he adapted some elements of classical tragedy to the English stage. The ten plays ascribed to Seneca were the accepted models of tragedy in the Renaissance. Their presentation of the more horrible stories of Greek tragedy, their rhetorical and aphoristic style, their moralizing and their psychology, were all greatly admired. They were believed by the Elizabethans to have been acted, and their murders and violence seemed

to warrant such action on the modern stage; though
the Elizabethans found less adaptable their use of the
chorus, the restriction of the number of persons speaking, their long monologues, and the limitation of the
action to the last phase of a story. Kyd modeled his
rhetoric on Seneca and retained a vestige of the chorus,
long soliloquies, and some other traits of Senecan
structure; but his main borrowing was the essential
story of a crime and its punishment. He thus brought
to the Elizabethan stage the classical theme of retribution. In his *Spanish Tragedy*, a murder is avenged
under the direction of a ghost, by a hesitating and solilo-
quizing protagonist, who is driven through doubt and
speculation almost to madness, and then to craft, with
which he outwits the wily villain and brings all the
leading *dramatis personæ* to a final slaughter.

Blood revenge was established as the favorite motive
of tragedy; the conflict of craft between protagonist
and villain made up the action, and the speculations of
the avenger gave a chance for wisdom and eloquence.
One other play, probably by Kyd, the lost *Hamlet*,
also presented these features and later formed the basis
for Shakespeare's tragedy. Other plays, as *Soliman
and Perseda*, *The True Tragedy of Richard III*, and
Locrine immediately adopted Kyd's theme and technic;
indeed the stage for half a dozen years abounded in
avenging heroes, diabolical villains, shrieking ghosts,
and long soliloquies on fate, death, retribution, and
kindred themes. *Titus Andronicus* is quite in the

Kydian vein. Many plays combined the salient traits of Marlowe and Kyd, and henceforth no one wrote tragedy without paying homage to their inventions.

We have now noticed the most important developments in comedy and tragedy made by the time that Shakespeare began writing for the theaters; and he made quick use of the progress accomplished by Plautian and Lylyan comedy, by Greene's romances, and by the tragedies of Kyd and Marlowe. There were other plays not easily classified under these names and of less service to Shakespeare. But to the critical playgoer of 1590 few plays would have seemed either 'right comedies' or 'right tragedies.' The majority were mere dramatizations of story without close construction or selection of material, seeking merely varied and abundant action. They drew their material from all kinds of narrative sources, Italian *novelle,* current pamphlets, Latin historians, or English chronicles; and, whether historical or fictitious, were usually known as Histories, *i.e.,* stories.

The patriotic interest in English history fostered the presentation of its scenes upon the stage. The chronicles of Halle and Holinshed furnished abundant material; and embassies, processions, and pitched battles filled the stage with movement. Historical plays might, indeed, draw from classical history or from current foreign history, but from 1590 to 1603 a very large number of plays give scenic representation to the reigns of English kings.

Some of these form a distinct class, since, however mixed with comic matter, they imitate Kyd or Marlowe and recast the chronicle of a reign to fit the accepted subjects of tragedy, the downfall of a prince, the revenge for a crime, the overthrow of a tyrant, or the retribution brought upon a conspirator or usurper. Conceived under Marlowe's influence, and perhaps owing something to his hand, is the tetralogy that includes the three parts of *Henry VI* and *Richard III*.

Those history plays, however, that do not follow the formulas for tragedy, are a heterogeneous group not easily classified. They usually keep to the loose chronicle method that presented a series of scenes without much regard to unity or coherence. Farce, comedy, magic, spectacle, heroics, and everything that might have happened was permissible in these plays, and perhaps the only thing indispensable was a pitched field with opposing armies. Biographical, comic, popular, patriotic, or what not, these plays brought a variety of scenes to the theaters, but offered only a loose and flexible form rather than any dramatic direction or model to the creator of Falstaff.

The early deaths of Greene and Marlowe and the retirement of Lyly left Shakespeare the heir of their inventions. Though his plays were at first imitative, he soon surpassed his predecessors in gift of expression, in depiction of character, and in deftness of dramatic technic. The years from 1593 to near the turn of the century are particularly lacking in records of plays or theaters; but it seems clear that the main developments of the drama were in romantic comedy and chronicle history; and it is also clear that Shakespeare was the unquestioned leader in both of these forms.

In comparison with his associates, he was now the master, relying on his own experience rather than on their innovations. Neither the crude but popular *Mucedorus* (1595) nor Dekker's poetical extravagance, *Old Fortunatus* (1596), could contribute to his development of romantic comedy; and domestic comedy could not instruct the inventor of Launce and Launcelot. Incidental relationships may indeed be noted. *As You Like It*, for example, dramatizes a pastoral novel with the addition of scenes that recall Robin Hood's forest life, and may owe something to the suggestion of two Robin Hood plays by Chettle and Munday, *The Downfall and Death of Robert Earl of Huntingdon* (1598). But, on the whole, the indebtedness was on the other side, and imitations indicate that men of Shakespeare's day realized that romantic comedy and history could not be carried farther.

In fact, a certain reaction set in against these forms of drama. Near the close of the century new tendencies became manifest. Comedy tended to become more realistic and satiric. Chapman, Marston, Middleton, and Jonson, all began writing romantic comedy, but changed shortly to realistic. Jonson, in his *Every Man in His Humour* (1598), announced his opposition to the lawless drama which had preceded — whether romantic comedy or chronicle history — and proposed the creation of a new satirical comedy of manners. He was moved partly by a desire to break from past methods in order to bring comedy closer to classical example, and partly by a desire for realism, a faithful presentation, analysis, and criticism of current manners. The growth of London and the increase in luxury and immorality seem to have encouraged such a movement, and for the decade after 1598 there were many comedies of London life, mostly satiric, and nearly all realistic. Many varieties are to be found, from gross representation of the seamy side of city life to serious discussion of social questions, and from sympathetic picturing of certain trades to satiric exposure of the evils of society.

Jonson's emulation of Aristophanes led him into arrogant personal satire in the *Poetaster* (1601), and there ensued the so-called war of the theaters, in which Marston, Dekker, and, according to report, Shakespeare were Jonson's opponents. If Shakespeare, indeed, had a share in this war, he showed only slight interest in the prevailing comedy. *Measure for Measure* uses the device of a spying duke employed in Marston's *Malcontent*, and discusses sexual relationships somewhat in the tone of the time, while the scenes dealing with houses of ill fame are not unlike similar scenes in the contemporary plays of Middleton, Webster, and others. *Troilus and Cressida*, also, show more of a satiric temper than is usual in Shakespeare. But neither of these plays partakes to any extent of the prevailing satire on contemporary London. Wide as was the range of Shakespeare's genius, it seems to have avoided the field of satire.

A review of the drama must, however, at least remark the importance of this development of realistic comedy which flourished in the decade after 1598 and continued to the end. Jonson's comedy of ' humors' includes *Volpone* (1605), which overstepped the bounds of comedy in its denunciation of evil, the *Alchemist* (1611), perhaps the best English play on the Latin model, and *Bartholomew Fair* (1614), most original and English of them all. Dekker's fine drama of middle class life, *The Honest Whore* (1604), and Heywood's masterpiece, *A Woman Killed with Kindness* (1603), a play suggesting both the sentimental comedy of the eighteenth century and the problem play of to-day, also belong to this very remarkable era of domestic themes and serious realism.

If Shakespeare did not turn to satire or realism or current social problems, he did turn away from chronicle history plays and romantic comedies. As we saw in the last chapter, for a period of eight or nine years, from *Julius Cæsar* to *Antony and Cleopatra*, he gave his best efforts of his maturity to tragedy. The day for mere imitation of Seneca, Kyd, or Marlowe, was past; and scholars like Jonson and Chapman as well as Shakespeare sought in the tragedy of the public theater an opportunity for wisdom and poetry and a criticism of life.

For models, Shakespeare did not need to go back farther than his own *Romeo and Juliet* and *Richard II*, nor to imitate any other than himself. Yet his great plays may have seemed to his contemporaries to adopt rather than to depart from current dramatic practices. They belong to the Elizabethan 'tragedy of blood'; against a background of courts and battles they present the downfall of princes; they rest on improbable stories that end in fearful slaughter; they invariably set forth great crimes, compact of murder, lust, villainous intrigue, and ferocious cruelty. Some of them follow Kyd in recounting a story of blood vengeance presided over by ghosts, or discover the retribution due for crime in physical torments. Nearly all follow Marlowe in centering the tragic interest in the fate of a supernormal protagonist who is swayed by an overpowering emotion, and in elevating these human desires and passions into tremendous forces that work their waste of devastation and ruin on character and life.

The contemporary tragedy is brought closest to Shakespeare in the relations of the revenge plays to *Hamlet*. The type, introduced by Kyd in *The Spanish Tragedy* and the original *Hamlet*, underwent a special development in Marston's *Antonio's Revenge* (1598) and several other plays appearing from 1598 to 1603, that dealt with the blood vengeance of a son for a father. At the same time Shakespeare turned to the

remaking of the old *Hamlet* and to a new treatment of
the old theme, yet retained many of the old accessories.
Marston reproduces the essential story of blood vengeance, presided over by a ghost, crossed by both lust
and sentimental love, commented on by long soliloquies,
and accompanied by pretended madness. Chettle, in
Hoffman, amplifies the horrors and villainy and brings
the story of the mad girl into closer juncture with the
main plot than is the case in *Hamlet*. Tourneur, writing
independently of Shakespeare, introduces, among all
sorts of horrors, a Christian ghost who forbids blood
vengeance and commands submission to Providence.
Ben Jonson, in his additions to the old *Spanish Tragedy*,
gives fine imaginative interpretation of the wavering
moods of meditation, irony, and frenzy with which
Kyd had dealt only crudely. The later development
of this type proceeded without much regard to Shakespeare's *Hamlet*, but rather in the direction started by
Marston's tragedies and his influential tragi-comedy,
The Malcontent. While *Hamlet* may be described as
centering attention on a meditative and high-minded
avenger, Tourneur, Webster, Middleton, and later
dramatists found greater interest in the study of villainy
and intrigue. Revenge is born of depravity rather than
duty, and given a setting of physical horrors and unnat-
ural lust. Tourneur's *Revenger's Tragedy* (1606) and
Webster's *White Devil* (1610) and *Duchess of Malfi* (1611)
represent the culmination of this drama of revenge, lust,
and horror, and supply a sort of standard for tragedy

until the Civil War. Webster, it must be added, was hardly less interested than Shakespeare in character and motive, though he chose to study these in a chamber of horrors.

Shakespeare's Roman tragedies also suggest comparison with contemporary plays, those either on Roman or on contemporary foreign history. Tragedies dealing with Roman history had preceded *Julius Cæsar*, but that play doubtless stimulated Jonson's *Sejanus* (1603) and *Catiline* (1611). Both these plays attempted an approach to classical structure and a thorough study and digest of classical history. This effort to make tragedy a serious and authoritative interpretation of history was also shared by Chapman in his plays dealing with contemporary French history, *1* and *2 Bussy D'Ambois* (1601–1607) and *1* and *2 Biron* (1608). While Jonson strove to free his style from the abundance of conceits, figures, and passages of description that had characterized earlier drama, Chapman used every chance to crowd his verse with far-stretched figure and weighty apothegm. At its worst it is peculiarly representative of Elizabethan confusion and bombast; at its best it is closest of all in its resemblance to Shakespeare's. Like Jonson and Chapman, Shakespeare sought historical backgrounds for his characters and found a fascination in the interpretation of the motives of the great protagonists of the world of antiquity. It is worthy of note, however, that he seems to have taken no interest in another class of subjects much favored by his contemporaries. Contemporary crimes treated with an excess of realism and didactic conclusions are common in drama from *Arden of Feversham* (1590) on, and engaged the services of Jonson, Webster, Ford, Dekker, and others.

About 1607 a new departure appeared in the work of the dramatic collaborators, Beaumont and Fletcher. After some experiments, they won, in their tragi-comedies, *Philaster* (1608) and *A King and No King* (1610), and their tragedy, *The Maid's Tragedy* (1609), great theatrical successes, and in these and similar plays established a new kind of dramatic romance. The realistic comedies of Jonson and Middleton, which, along with the great tragedies of Shakespeare, crowd the stage history of the preceding ten years, had offered nothing similar to these romances which joined tragic and idyllic material in scenes of brilliant theatrical effectiveness, abounding in transitions from suspense to surprise, and culminating in telling dénouements. This new realm of romance is an artificial one, contrasting pure love with horrid entanglements of lust, and ever bringing love in conflict with duty, friendship, or the code of honor. In its intriguing courts, or in nearby forests where the idyls are placed, love of one kind or another is the ruling and vehement passion, riding high-handed over tottering thrones, rebellious subjects, usurping tyrants, and checked, if checked at all, only by the unexampled force of honor. Romance, in short, depends on situation, on the artificial but skilful juxtaposition of emotions and persons, and on the new technic that sacrifices consistency of characterization for surprise. Characterization tends to become typical, and motives tend to be based on fixed conventions, such as the code of honor might dictate to a seventeenth-century gentleman; but the lack of individuality in character is counterbalanced by the vividness with which the lovers, tyrants, faithful friends, evil women, and sentimental heroines are presented, and by the fluent and lucid style which varies to any emotional requirement and rises to the demands of the most sensational situations.

Cymbeline in its plot bears some close resemblances to *Philaster*, and it seems likely that Shakespeare was adopting the methods and materials of the new romance. At all events, he turned from tragedy to romance, and in *Cymbeline* and the far more original and successful *Winter's Tale* and *Tempest* produced tragi-comedies that, like Beaumont and Fletcher's, rely on a contrast of tragic and idyllic and on surprising plots and idealized heroines. After Beaumont's retirement in 1611 or 1612, it seems probable that Fletcher and Shakespeare collaborated together on *Henry VIII* and *The Two Noble Kinsmen*.

There is ample evidence that the plays of Beaumont and Fletcher won a great popular renown, surpassing for a time those of Shakespeare and all others. Beaumont did not live long after he ceased to write for the stage, dying at thirty, in the same year as Shakespeare. Jonson had given up dramatic writing for the time, and Fletcher was left the chief writer for Shakespeare's old company and the undoubted leader of the theater. Including the plays written in collaboration with Beaumont, Shakespeare, and later with Massinger, he left some sixty dramas of many kinds, varying from farcical comedy of manners to the most extreme tragedy. The comedies of manners present the affairs of women, and spice their lively conversation and surprising situations with a wit that often reminds one of the Restoration; indeed they carry the development of comedy nearly to the point where Wycherley and Congreve began. The tragi-comedies, which display the qualities already noted as belonging to the romances, have the technical advantage that the disentanglement of their rapid plots and sub-plots is left hanging in the balance until the very end. The happy ending to tragic entanglements won a favor it has never lost on the English stage, and tragi-comedy of the Fletcherian type continued the most popular form of the drama until Dryden.

It is unnecessary here to dwell long over the drama after Shakespeare's death. Jonson, Dekker, Heywood, and Webster wrote from time to time, and Middleton devoted his versatile talent to whatever kind of play was in vogue, now rather to Websterian tragedy and Fletcherian tragi-comedy than to realistic comedy. Yet, in collaboration with Rowley, he produced the powerful tragedy, *The Changeling*, and the much-admired tragi-comedy, *A Fair Quarrel*. After Fletcher's death in 1625, Massinger took his place as leader of the stage, and his work, with that of Ford and Shirley, carry on the great traditions of the drama to the very end. A host of minor writers, as Brome, D'Avenant, Suckling, Cartwright, offer little that is new; but no survey of the drama, however brief, can neglect to mention the skilful exposition, admirable psychology, and sound structural principles that characterized the best of Massinger's many plays, the unique and amazing dramatic genius shown in Ford's masterpieces, *The Broken Heart* and *'Tis Pity She's a Whore*, and the ingenuity in plot, adroitness in characterization, and genuine poetic gifts of Shirley.

Comedies from 1616 to 1642 reveal two chief influences; they are realistic and satiric, following Jonson, or they are light-hearted, lively combinations of manners and intrigue, after Fletcher. In the former class are Massinger's two great comedies, *The City Madam* and *A New Way to Pay Old Debts*. To the latter class belong most of the comedies of Shirley. Tragi-comedies follow Fletcher with the variations due to the authors' ingenuity, and include perhaps the most attractive plays of Massinger and Shirley. Tragedies usually mingle lust, devilish intrigue, physical horror, after the fashion of Webster and Tourneur, but now often with romantic variation on the theme of love, and a technic of suspense and surprise similar to Beaumont and Fletcher. These are the main tendencies in the last twenty years of the drama, and characterize in the large the work of the greater men as well as of the less. Shakespeare's influence is widespread, but appears incidentally in particular scene, situation, character, or phrase, rather than as affecting the main course and fashions of the drama. After the publication of his plays in 1623, this incidental influence increased, and is distinctly noticeable in the plays of Ford and Shirley.

A glance must suffice for two dramatic forms that had only slight connection with the public theaters, the Pastoral Play and the Court Masque. Pastoral elements are found in many early entertainments and in the plays of Lyly and Peele. Later, in imitation of Guarini's *Il Pastor Fido*, attempts were made to inaugurate a pastoral drama, presenting a full-fledged dramatic exposition of the golden age. Daniel's *Queen's Arcadia* (1605) and Fletcher's *Faithful Shepherdess* (1609) had many later followers, but the form won no permanent hold on the popular taste. Traces of its influence, however, may often be seen, as in Shakespeare's *As You Like It*, or Beaumont and Fletcher's *Philaster*. The masque, originally only a masquerade, soon acquired some dramatic accompaniment, and in the court of James I developed into an elaborate form of entertainment. The masked dance of the ladies and gentlemen of the court was merely the focus for dialogue, elaborate setting, spectacle, music, and grotesque dances by professionals. These shows, costing vast sums for staging, costumes, and music,

I

depended for their success mainly on the architect Inigo
Jones, but in some degree also on Ben Jonson, who was
the creator of the Court Masque as a literary form.
Such expensive spectacles were far beyond the reach
of the public theater, but provoked considerable imitation, as in Shakespeare's *Tempest*, or several of Beaumont and Fletcher's plays.   Later Milton immortalized
the form in *Comus*.

The most hasty review of the Elizabethan drama
must suggest how constantly Shakespeare responded to
its prevailing conditions.   There are, of course, great
variations in the signs which different plays offer
of contemporary influence and peculiarity.   So it is
with most of his fellow dramatists.   *Lear* and *Othello*
were perhaps written within the same year, yet *Othello*,
in its unity, its technical excellence, and its depiction of
character, is the most modern of the tragedies, while
Lear, with its impossible story, its horrors, its treatment
of madness, its likeness to the chronicle plays, its prolonged passage from crisis to catastrophe, in its very
conception, is the most Elizabethan, though perhaps
the most impressive of the tragedies.   *Twelfth Night* is
suited to any stage, but *Troilus and Cressida* and *Pericles*
are hardly conceivable except on the Elizabethan.   Despite such variations, however, Shakespeare's relations
to the contemporary drama were manifestly constant
and immediate.   If it was rarely a question with him
what the ancients had written, it was always a question
what was being acted and what was successful at the

moment. His own growth in dramatic power goes step by step with the rapid and varied development of the drama, and the measure for comparison must be, not by decades, but by years or months.

A study of the Elizabethan drama may help to excuse some of the faults and limitations of Shakespeare, but it also enforces his merits. Both faults and merits are often to be understood in the efforts of lesser men to do what he did. We admire his triumphs the more as we consider their failures. Yet they often had admirable success, and their triumphs as well as his are due in part to the dramatic conditions which gave the freest opportunity for individual initiative in language, verse, story, and construction. Noble bursts of poetry, richness and variety of life, an intense interest in human nature, comic or tragic — these are the great merits of that drama. That in a superlative degree they are also the characteristics of Shakespeare is not due solely to his exceptional genius, but to the fact that his genius worked in a favorable environment.

A TYPICAL SHAKESPEREAN STAGE

From Albright's *Shaksperian Stage*

CHAPTER VI

The Elizabethan Theater

In 1576, James Burbage, father of the great actor, Richard Burbage, and himself a member of the Earl of Leicester's company, built the first London playhouse, the Theater in Shoreditch. In the next year a second playhouse, the Curtain, was erected nearby, and these seem to have remained the only theaters until 1587–1588, when probably the Rose, on the Bankside, was built by Henslowe. In 1599 Richard and Cuthbert Burbage, after some difficulty over their lease, demolished the old Theater and used the timber for the Globe, near the Rose, on the Bankside. The Swan, another theater, had been built there in 1594, somewhat to the west; and in 1614 the Hope was erected hard by the old Rose and the new Globe, which in 1613 had replaced the old Globe. Meantime the Fortune had been built by Henslowe and Alleyn in 1600 in Golden Lane to the north of Cripplegate, on the model of the Globe, and the Red Bull was erected in the upper end of St. John's Street about 1603–1607. These were all public theaters, open to the air, built of wood, outside the city limits and the jurisdiction of the city corporation.

Before the Theater, plays had been acted in various places about the city, and especially in inn-yards, some of which long continued to be used for dramatic performances.   At an early date also, the companies of children actors connected with the choirs of St. Paul's and the Queen's Chapel had given public performances, probably indoors, at places near St. Paul's and in Blackfriars.   When the Burbages were in difficulties about the Theater, they had leased certain rooms in the dismantled monastery of Blackfriars, but had then released these to a company of children which acted there for some years.   In 1608 the Burbages regained possession of this property, and Shakespeare's company began acting there.   This Blackfriars theater was known as a private theater in order to avoid the application of certain statutes directed against the public theaters, but it differed from them merely in being indoors, with artificial lights, and higher prices.   It was used by Shakespeare's company as a winter theater, while the Globe served for summer performances, and it was the model for various other private theaters, two of which survived the Protectorate and became in turn the models for the Restoration Theater.   Drury Lane and Covent Garden, indeed, trace their ancestry back directly to the Blackfriars through the Cockpit and the Salisbury Court playhouses.

The companies of actors which occupied these theaters were coöperative organizations.   Eight or ten actors formed a company, leased a theater, hired super-

numeraries, bought plays, and shared in the profits.
In Elizabeth's reign they secured a legal position by
obtaining a license from some nobleman, and so were
known as the Earl of Leicester's men, Lord Admiral's
men, and so on. On the accession of James I, the leading London companies were taken directly under
patronage of members of the royal family. During
Shakespeare's time there were innumerable companies,
but the tendency was for the best actors to become
associated in a few companies, and for each company
to keep to a particular theater; so that at the accession of James I, there were only five adult companies in
London with permanent theaters. The best companies
were frequently employed to act at court, and during
the summer or when the plague was raging in London,
they often toured the country. The children's companies flourished from time to time, and especially
from 1599–1607 they were, as we learn from *Hamlet*,
formidable rivals of the men.

The history of the adult companies shows the growth
of two distinct interests, that of Henslowe and Alleyn,
and that of the Burbages. Henslowe, whose diary is
one of the chief documents for the history of the
theater, built the Rose, and in partnership with his
son-in-law, the famous actor Alleyn, controlled the
Fortune and the Hope, and the companies known as
the Admiral's and the Earl of Worcester's men, and
later on the Queen's and the Prince's men. The Burbages owned the Theater, the Globe, and the Blackfriars,

and were in control of Shakespeare's company. This company, at first the Earl of Leicester's men, was known by the names of its various patrons, Strange's, Derby's, Hunsdon's, and the Lord Chamberlain's, until in 1603 it became the King's men. For a short time, as Lord Strange's men, it acted at the Rose, and apparently later at the playhouse in Newington Butts, but its regular theaters were the Theater, the Globe, and Blackfriars. With this company Shakespeare was connected from the beginning, and he aided in making it the chief London company. For a time, Alleyn and the Admiral's men were its close rivals, but even before the accession of James I, Shakespeare and Burbage had given it a supremacy that it maintained to the closing of the theaters.

There are various pictures of the exterior of Elizabethan theaters in the contemporary maps or views of London, the best representation of the four Bankside theaters being the engraving of Hollar printed in the Tudor edition of *Twelfth Night*. This was first published in *Londinopolis*, 1657, but represents the Bankside as it was about 1620. Four pictures of interiors have been preserved, that from Kirkman's *Drolls*, those from the title-pages of *Roxana* and *Messalina*, and the DeWitt drawing of the Swan, reproduced in the Tudor Shakespeare, *1 Henry VI*. The drawing from Kirkman's *Drolls* is usually known as the Red Bull stage, but it was not issued until 1679, and does not seem to have anything to do with the Red Bull or with any other regular theater. The *Messalina* and *Roxana* pictures are small, and both show a rear curtain and a projecting stage. The DeWitt drawing was done from hearsay evidence, is inaccurate in details, and represents a theater with a movable stage, probably not long regularly used for plays; it gives little idea of the stage, but does afford a good general notion of the interior of a public theater. The contract for the Fortune theater, built on the model of the Globe, except that it was square instead of octagonal, has been preserved and enables us to complete this view of the interior in detail.

The public theaters were usually round, or nearly round, wooden buildings of three stories. These stories were occupied by tiers of galleries encircling the pit, which was open to the air. The stage projected halfway into the pit, and was provided with dressing rooms in the rear, and a protecting roof overhead, supported in some cases by pillars. At the top was the 'hut', a room used to provide apparatus for raising and lowering persons or properties from the stage. Light when needed was provided by torches. Admission to standing room in the pit was usually only a penny, but seats in the gallery or boxes or on the stage cost much more, rising as high as half a crown. Performances were given on every fair day except Sunday, and a flag flying from the hut indicated that a play was to be performed. Some of the public playhouses were used for acrobats, fencing, or even bear-baiting as well as for plays; but the better theaters, as the Globe and Fortune, seem to have been limited to dramatic performances.

The size and arrangement of the stage doubtless varied somewhat with the different theaters, and considerable changes seem to have been introduced by the indoor private theaters. But the Curtain was used from 1577 to 1642, some new theaters were modeled closely on the old, and the same plays were acted on different stages, so it is apparent that in all the stage was the same in its main features. For clearness these may be again enumerated. The stage was a platform projecting into the pit, open on three sides, and without any front curtain. In the rear were two doors, and between them, an alcove, or inner stage, separated from the front stage by curtains. Above the inner stage was a gallery, also provided with curtains, and over the doors were windows or balconies. The arrangement of doors, inner stage, gallery, and curtain may have varied somewhat, but the essential elements are a curtained space at the rear, and a gallery above. Trap-doors were also provided, and the hut overhead supplied the machinery for ascents and descents of gods and goddesses.

Our diagram for the ground floor of the Fortune shows a square-cornered stage with doors flat on the rear, while the perspective drawing from Dr. Albright's *Shaksperian Stage* shows a tapering stage, as in the *Messalina* picture, with doors on the bias. Some stages

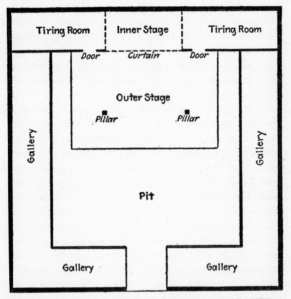

GROUND PLAN OF THE FORTUNE THEATER

Dimensions: 80 ft. square on the outside; 55 ft. square on the inside the stage 43 ft. wide and extending to the middle of the pit.

may have had rounded corners with doors in the sides. The pillars were not necessary in the private theaters; or in some public houses where other means were found for supporting the roof.

The performance of a play differed in many ways from one to-day. There was no scenery and there were no women actors. Though scenes were used in court performances as early as 1604, they do not seem to have been employed by the professional companies to any extent until after the Restoration. Female parts were taken by boys, and, except in plays acted by the children's companies, there were rarely more than two important female characters in a play. Though without scenery, the Elizabethan stage was by no means devoid of spectacle. Processions, battles, all kinds of mythological beings, ascents to heaven, descents to hell, fireworks, and elaborate properties, were employed. Numerous contemporary plays indicate that neither the fairyland of *A Midsummer-Night's Dream*, nor the magnificent court of *Henry VIII*, was devised without an eye to the resources of the stage. Large sums of money were lavished on costumes, the cost of a coat often exceeding the price paid an author for a play. Costume was anachronistic; Cleopatra was impersonated by a boy in stays and farthingale; and Cæsar, probably by Burbage, in a costume much like that worn by the Earl of Essex. Some attention, however, was paid to appropriateness. Shepherds were clothed in white, hunters in green; and doubtless mermaids,

fairies, Venuses, and satyrs were given as appropriate
a dress as fancy could devise. The action of a play
seems usually to have been completed in two hours.
There was sometimes music between the acts, but
there were no long waits, and little stage business.

The peculiarities in the presentation of a play due
to the arrangement of the stage were considerable, and
have been the subject of much discussion and mis-
understanding among investigators. There is, however, no doubt that the action was largely on the front
stage, and that most of the scenes, at least in Shakespeare's lifetime, were designed for presentation on this
projecting platform. Since there was no drop-curtain,
actors had some distance to traverse, on entrances and
exits, between the doors and the front. At the end of a
scene or a play, all must retire, and the bodies of the
dead must be carried out. Hence a tragedy often
ends with a funeral procession, a comedy with a dance.
The indications of scene supplied by modern editors
for Shakespeare's plays help to visualize a modern
presentation, but are misleading as to Shakespeare's
intentions or an Elizabethan performance. The majority of scenes in his plays differ strikingly from those
in a modern play in that they offer no hints as to the
exact locality. Often it is not clear from the text
whether the scene is conceived as indoors or outdoors,
in the palace, or the courtyard, or before the entrance.
Even when the scene is presumably within a room,
there is often no indication of the nature of the furnish-

ings, never any of the elaborate attention to details of setting, such as we find in a play by Pinero or Shaw. Sometimes placards were hung up indicating the scene of a play, but apparently these merely gave the general scene, as "Venice" or "Verona," and did not often designate localities more closely. In fact the majority of the scenes were probably written with no precise conception of their setting. They were written to be acted on a front stage, bare of scenery, projecting out into the audience. This did not represent a particular locality, but rather any locality whatever.

The inner stage and the gallery above, and to some extent the doors and the windows, were used to indicate specific localities when these were necessary. The gallery represented the wall of a town, an upper story of a house, or any elevated locality. The doors represented doors to houses or gates to a city, and the windows or balconies over them were often used for the windows of the houses. The inner stage was used in various ways to indicate a specific locality requiring properties, and this use apparently increased as time went on, and especially in the indoor, artificially lighted private theaters. In any case, however, when the curtains were opened, the inner stage became a part of the main stage, and while action might take place there, it might also serve as a background for action proceeding in the front. Properties could be brought on and off the inner stage behind the closed curtains, hence large properties were confined to its precincts.

Furniture, as chairs, tables, or even beds, could, however, be pushed or carried out from the inner to the outer stage. A play might be given on the front stage without using the curtained recess at all, but numerous references to curtains make it clear that the inner stage was used from the early days of the theater.

The uses of the inner stage have been much discussed and are still in dispute, but they may be summarized briefly. *First*, the inner stage was used for a specific, restricted, and usually propertied locality — a cave, a study, a shop, a prison. *Second*, the inner stage was used for scenes requiring discovery or tableaux. Numerous stage directions indicate the drawing of the curtains to present a scene set on the inner stage, as Bethsabe at her bath, Friar Bungay in bed with his magical apparatus about him, Ferdinand and Miranda playing chess. *Third*, the use of the inner stage was extended so that it represented any propertied background, especially for scenes in a forest, church, or temple. In *As You Like It*, for example, the last four acts are located in the Forest of Arden. "This is the Forest of Arden," says Rosalind as soon as she arrives there; and even before this, Duke senior alludes to "these woods," and later we learn that there are practicable trees on which Orlando hangs his verses. The forest setting, consisting of trees and rocks, was placed on the inner stage and served to give a scenic background. Of course, different places in the forest are to be presumed, but one forest background would be sufficient for all. In the course of the four acts, however, there are three scenes (II. ii; II. iii; III. i) that are not in the forest, but at unspecified and unpropertied places about the palace and Oliver's house. For these scenes the curtain would be closed, shutting off the forest background and transferring the spectators to the unspecified localities of Act I, *i.e.*, to the bare front stage. *Fourth.* An extension of this last use made it possible to employ the curtain to indicate change of scene. Several scenes, where no heavy properties were required, might succeed one another on the front stage with the curtains closed; but the opening of the curtains would reveal a special background and a manifest change of scene. One instance of this use of the inner stage is seen in the immediate change from an outdoor to an indoor scene, or *vice versa*. The scene is in the street, *i.e.*, on the front stage; the person knocks at one of the doors and is admitted to a house; when he reappears, it is through the inner stage, the curtains of which have been drawn, disclosing the setting of a room. Or this process is reversed. In *A Yorkshire Tragedy*, there is an interesting case of such an alternation from indoors to outdoors, with one character remaining on the stage all of the time. A more extensive use of this "alternation" could be employed to indicate marked changes of place. As long as the action remains in Venice, the bare front stage will do, but a transfer to Portia's house at Belmont can be made by means of the curtains and the inner stage.

In the later plays at the private theaters this use of the inner stage, then better lighted, seems to have increased, especially in the change from a street or general hall to special apartments.

These uses of the inner stage, together with that of the upper stage or gallery, gave a chance for considerable variety in the action, and rendered the rapid succession of scenes less bewildering than one would at first suppose. Shakespeare's stage was the outcome of the peculiar conditions of acting by professionals in the sixteenth century, but it was also a natural step in the evolution from the medieval to the modern stage. On the medieval stage there was a neutral place or *platea* and special localized and propertied places called *sedes, domus, loca*. On the Elizabethan stage the front stage is the *platea*, the inner and upper stages the *domus* or *loca*. In the Restoration theater the scenery was placed on the inner stage and shut off from the outer stage by a curtain. With the use of scenery, the inner stage became more important, and the projecting apron of the front stage was gradually cut down. The proscenium doors in front of the curtain long survived their original use as entrances, but, as a rule, they have now finally disappeared with the front stage. The modern picture-frame stage of to-day is the evolution of the inner stage of the Elizabethans. Similarly the method of stage presentation has changed only gradually from Shakespeare's day to ours. The alternation from outer to inner stage was very common

K

in the Restoration theaters, where flat scenes were used instead of a curtain, and it may still be seen in the production of melodrama or of Shakespeare's plays. A painted drop shuts off a few feet of the stage, which becomes a street or a hall, while properties and scenery are being arranged in the rear. When the drop goes up, we pass from the street or the court of the wicked Duke to the Forest of Arden, just as the Elizabethans did.

The Elizabethan stage affected Shakespeare's dramatic art in many ways. The absence of scenery, of women actors, and of a front curtain, the use of a bare stage that served for neutral or unspecified localities, naturally influenced the composition of every play. But the theatrical presentation was by no means as crude or as medieval as these differences from modern practice seem to indicate. The intimacy established between actors and audience by the projecting stage, the rapidity of action hastened by the lack of scenery or furniture, the possibilities of rapid changes of scene rendered intelligible by the use of the inner stage, were all manifest advantages in encouraging dramatic invention. The traditions formed in this theater for the presentation of *Hamlet, Romeo and Juliet,* and the other plays, were handed on from Shakespeare and Burbage to Lowin and Taylor, to Betterton, Cibber, and Garrick, down to the present day; and have perhaps been less revolutionized by scenery and electric lights than we might imagine.

CHAPTER VII

THE TEXT OF SHAKESPEARE

THE main difficulties that stand in the way of determining the actual form in which Shakespeare left his plays are due, first, to the total absence of manuscripts, and, secondly, to the fact that he, like his contemporaries, regarded dramatic literature as material for performance on the stage, not as something to be read in the library. The most obvious evidence of this lies in his having himself issued with every appearance of personal attention his poems of *Venus and Adonis* and *Lucrece*, while he permitted his plays to find their way into print without any trace of supervision and, in some cases, apparently without his consent. When the author sold a play to the theatrical company which was to perform it, he appears to have regarded himself as having no longer any rights in it; and when a play was published, we are in general justified in supposing either that it had been obtained surreptitiously, or that it had been disposed of by the company. Exceptions to this begin to appear in the first half of the seventeenth century, notably in the case of Heywood, who defended his action on the plea of protecting the text from mutilation, and in that of Ben Jonson, who issued

131

in 1616, in the face of ridicule for his presumption, a folio volume of his "Works." But, though Shakespeare is reported to have felt annoyance at the pirating of his productions, there is no evidence of his having been led to protect himself or the integrity of his writings by departing from the usual practice in his profession.

Among the various documents which make us aware of this situation, so general then, but so strongly in contrast with modern methods, three explicit statements by Heywood are so illuminating that they deserve quotation. One occurs in the preface to his *Rape of Lucrece*, 1608:

To the Reader. — It hath beene no custome in mee of all other men (courteous Reader) to commit my plaies to the presse: the reason though some may attribute to my owne insufficiencie, I had rather subscribe in that to their seuare censure then by seeking to auoide the imputation of weaknes to incurre greater suspistion of honestie: for though some haue vsed a double sale of their labours, first to the Stage, and after to the presse, For my owne part I heere proclaime my selfe euer faithfull in the first, and neuer guiltie of the last: yet since some of my plaies haue (vnknowne to me, and without any of my direction) accidentally come into the Printers hands, and therefore so corrupt and mangled, (copied only by the eare) that I haue bin as vnable to know them, as ashamed to chalenge them, This therefore, I was the willinger to furnish out in his natiue habit: first being by consent, next because the rest haue beene so wronged in being publisht in such sauadge and ragged ornaments: accept it courteous Gentlemen, and prooue as fauorable Readers as we haue found you gratious Auditors. Yours T. H.

The second is in Heywood's *Pleasant Dialogues and Dramas*, 1637, the prologue to *If you know not me, you know no bodie; Or, The troubles of Queen Elizabeth*. It is as follows:

A Prologve to the Play of Queene Elizabeth as it was last revived at the Cock-pit, in which the Author taxeth the most corrupted copy now imprinted, which was published without his consent.

PROLOGUE

Playes have a fate in their conception lent,
Some so short liv'd, no sooner shew'd than spent;
But borne to-day, to morrow buried, and
Though taught to speake, neither to goe nor stand.
This: (by what fate I know not) sure no merit,
That it disclaimes, may for the age inherit.
Writing 'bove one and twenty: but ill nurst,
And yet receiv'd as well perform'd at first,
Grac't and frequented, for the cradle age,
Did throng the Seates, the Boxes, and the Stage
So much: that some by Stenography drew
The plot: put it in print: (scarce one word trew:)
And in that lamenesse it hath limp't so long,
The Author now to vindicate that wrong
Hath tooke the paines, upright upon its feete
To teache it walke, so please you sit, and see't.

The third passage occurs in the address to the reader prefixed to *The English Traveller*, 1633:

True it is that my plays are not exposed to the world in volumes, to bear the titles of Works (as others). One reason is that many of them by shifting and changing of companies have been negligently lost; others of them are still retained in the hands of some actors who think it against their peculiar profit to have them come in print; and a third that it was never any great ambition in me in this kind to be voluminously read.

From these passages we gather that Heywood considered it dishonest to sell the same play to the stage and to the press; that some of his plays were stolen through stenographic reports taken in the theater and were printed in corrupt forms; that, in order to counteract this, he obtained the consent of the theatrical owners to his publication of a correct edition; that some actors considered the printing of plays against their interest (presumably because they thought that if a man could read a play, he would not care to see it acted); and that many plays were lost through negligence and the changes in the theatrical companies.   That we are here dealing with the conditions of Shakespeare's time is clear enough, since the edition of *If you know not me* on which Heywood casts reflections was published in 1605, and in 1604 Marston supplies corroboration in the preface to his *Malcontent*:

I would fain leave the paper; only one thing afflicts me, to think that scenes, invented merely to be spoken, should be enforcively published to be read, and that the least hurt I can receive is to do myself the wrong.   But since others otherwise would do me more, the least inconvenience is to be accepted. I have myself, therefore, set forth this comedy; but so, that my enforced absence must much rely upon the printer's discretion : but I shall entreat slight errors in orthography may be as slightly overpassed, and that the unhandsome shape which this trifle in reading presents, may be pardoned for the pleasure it once afforded you when it was presented with the soul of lively action.

The only form in which any of Shakespeare's plays found their way into print during his lifetime was that of small pamphlets, called Quartos, which were sold at sixpence each. In the case of five of these there is general agreement that they came to the press by the surreptitious method of reporting described by Heywood: the first Quarto versions of *Romeo and Juliet*, *Henry V*, *The Merry Wives*, *Hamlet*, and *Pericles*. Minute study of these texts has led to many ingenious explanations of their origin, including reports by memory from someone connected with the company, assembling of actors' parts or other portions of the playhouse text as well as reports by stenography or otherwise from a note-taker in the theater. The methods of reporting seem to have differed somewhat with each play, but Heywood's general description applies to all of these quartos — " accidentally come into the printer's hands," "corrupt and mangled," "copied only by the ear." The first Quartos of *Richard III* and *King Lear*, though much superior to the five mentioned, yet contain so many variants from the text of the Folio which seem to be due to mistakes of the ear and to slips of memory, that possibly they should also be included.

Redress for such pirating as is implied in these publications was difficult on account of the absence of a law of copyright. The chief pieces of legislation affecting the book trade were the law of licensing and the charter of the Stationers' Company. According to the first, all books, with a few exceptions, such as academic publications, had to be licensed before publication. The Stationers' Company, a close corporation of printers and publishers, exercised its powers for the protection of its members rather than of authors. A publisher wishing to establish a monopoly in a book he had acquired entered it on the Stationers' Register, paying a fee of sixpence, and was thereby protected against piracy. When the copy so registered was improperly acquired, the state of the case is not so clear. At times the officials showed hesitation about registering a book until the applicant "hath gotten sufficient authoritye for yt," and *As You Like It*, for example, appears in the Register only "to be staied," which it was until the publication of the first Folio. Further, the pirated *Romeo and Juliet* and *Henry V* were never entered at all; the pirated *Hamlet* and *Pericles* were entered, but to other publishers, who in the case of *Hamlet* brought out a more correct text in the following year; the pirated *Merry Wives* was transferred from one publisher to another on the day of entry, and actually issued by the second. Thus this group of plays does not support the view that the Stationers' Company stood ready to give perpetual copyright to their members even for obviously stolen goods. It is to be noted, too, that the previous publication of these surreptitious copies formed no hindrance to the later issue of an authentic copy. The second Quarto of *Hamlet*, printed from a complete manuscript, followed, as has been said, the first the next year, and the same thing happened in the case of *Romeo and Juliet*.

On the other hand, the great majority of the Quartos printed from playhouse copies of the plays were regularly entered, and the rights of the original publisher preserved to him. The appearance of groups of plays in the market following interference with theatrical activity such as came from the plague in 1594, from the breaking up of companies, or from Puritan attempts at restriction, confirm the belief that these better Quartos were honorably acquired by the publishers from the companies owning them, when the actors thought that there was more to gain than to lose by giving them to tne press.

The accompanying "Table of Quarto Editions" gives the names of all the Shakespearean plays issued in this form before the publication of the collected edition in 1623, known as the First Folio. In the cases of *Romeo and Juliet*, *1 Henry IV*, *Love's Labour's Lost*, *Merchant of Venice*, *Much Ado*, *A Midsummer-Night's Dream*, and *Richard II*, a Quarto, usually the most recent, provided the text from which the version in the Folio was printed. Hence, though in several cases the copy of the Quarto thus employed seems to have been one used by the actors and containing corrections of some value, the extant Quarto rather than the

TABLE OF QUARTO EDITIONS BEFORE 1623

	Entries in Stationers' Register	Dates of						Source of Q Text	Source of F1 Text
		Q1	Q2	Q3	Q4	Q5	Q6		
T.A.	Feb. 6, 1594	1594	1600	1611				Playhouse	Q3 completed and corrected
R. II	Aug. 29, 1597	1597	1598	1608	1615	1612		Playhouse	Q4 corrected
R. III	Oct. 19, 1597	1597	1598	1602	1605		1622	Disputed	Disputed
R. J.	No entry	1597	1599	1609	n. d.			Q1 Reported / Q2 Playhouse	Q3 from Q2
1 H. IV	Feb. 25, 1598	1598	1599	1604	1608	1613	1622	Playhouse	Q5 corrected
L. L. L.	No entry	1598						Playhouse	Q1
Merch.	July 22, 1598 (conditional) Oct. 28, 1600	1600	1600 or 1619					Playhouse	Q1 (Heyes)

						Reported	Independent
H. V .	[Aug. 4, 1600] "to be stayed"	1600	1602	{1608 or 1619}		Reported	Independent
M. Ado	[Aug. 4, 1600] "to be stayed"	1600				Playhouse	Q₁ corrected
2 H. IV	Aug. 23, 1600 / Aug. 23, 1600	1600	1600			Playhouse	Independent
M.N.D.	Oct. 8, 1600	1600	{1600 or 1619}			Playhouse	Q₂ corrected
M. W.	Jan. 18, 1602	1602	1619			Reported	Independent
Hml.	July 26, 1602	1603	1604, 5	1611		{ Q₁ Reported / Q₂ Playhouse	Independent
Lear	Nov. 26, 1607	1608	{1608 or 1619}			Disputed	Disputed (Q₁ in several states)
T. C.	Feb. 7, 1603 (conditional) / Jan. 28, 1609	1609	1609		1619	Playhouse	Independent (Q₁ in two issues)
Per.	May 20, 1608	1609	1609	1611	1619	Reported	Not in F₁ / F₂ from Q₄
Oth.	Oct. 6, 1621	1622				Playhouse	Independent

Folio is the prime authority for the text to-day. The same is true of *Titus Andronicus*, except that in this case the Folio restores from some manuscript source a scene which had been dropped from the Quarto.   If, as some hold, the Folio texts of *Richard III* and *King Lear* were printed from Quartos, there must have been available also a manuscript version, which is so heavily drawn upon that the Folio text virtually represents an independent source, as it does in the case of four of the five plays acknowledged to be due to surreptitious reporting.   *Pericles*, the fifth of these, was first admitted to the collected works in the third Folio, and is the only "reported" text forming our sole authority.

In the table of Quarto editions may be noted four entries with the words "or 1619" added to the date which appears on the title-page.   These four plays, along with the 1619 Quartos of *The Merry Wives* and *Pericles*, an undated Quarto of *The Whole Contention* (the earlier form of *2* and *3 Henry VI*), the Quarto of *Sir John Oldcastle*, dated 1600, and the Quarto of *A Yorkshire Tragedie*, dated 1619, have been shown by Mr. A. W. Pollard, with the coöperation of Mr. W. W. Greg, to have been put on the market at the same time, and Mr. W. J. Neidig has proved from typographical evidence that the title-pages of all nine were set up in succession in 1619.   It now seems established that in the case of these nine Quartos the correct date of publication should be 1619, and that, in the case of *The Merchant* and *A Midsummer-Night's Dream* the question of the comparative authority of the Heyes and Fisher Quartos respectively as against that of the Roberts Quartos should be settled against the latter. This last point is the only part of this remarkable discovery which is of importance in determining the text, as the Quartos dated 1608 and 1619 were already known to be mere reprints of earlier ones.

We come now to the publication of the First Folio, the most important single volume in the history of the text of Shakespeare. On November 8, 1623, the following entry occurs in the Stationers' Register:

Mr. Blount: Isaak Jaggard. Entred for their copie under, the hands of Mr Doctor Worrall and Mr Cole, Warden Mr William Shakspeers Comedyes, Histories and Tragedyes, soe manie of the said copyes as are not formerly entred to other men vizt, Comedyes. The Tempest. The two gentlemen of Verona. Measure for Measure. The Comedy of Errors. As you like it. All's well that ends well. Twelft Night. The winters tale. Histories. The thirde part of Henry the sixt. Henry the eight. Tragedies. Coriolanus. Timon of Athens. Julius Cæsar. Mackbeth. Anthonie and Cleopatra. Cymbeline.

One notes here the omission of *1* and *2 Henry VI, King John,* and *The Taming of the Shrew,* which had neither been previously entered nor issued in Quarto. This is probably due to the fact that three of these are based on older plays of which Quartos exist, which may have seemed to the publishers reason enough to save their sixpences. If we assume that "The thirde part of Henry the sixt" is a misprint for "The first part," the explanation covers the whole case. The registration of *Antony and Cleopatra* was superfluous, as it had been entered, though not printed, so far as we know, on May 20, 1608.

There are thus in the First Folio, the publication of which immediately followed this entry in 1623, twenty plays not before issued, for which the text of this volume is our sole authority. The emphasis so commonly placed on the supreme value of the text of the First Folio is justified with regard to these twenty plays; as for the remaining seventeen, its importance is shared, in proportions varying from play to play, with the texts of the Quartos. The sources from which the compilers of the Folio obtained their new material were in all probability playhouse copies, as in the case of the better Quartos. Heminge and Condell, Shakespeare's actor colleagues and friends, who sign the Address to the Readers, would obviously be the instruments for obtaining such copies. As for the so-called "private transcripts" which some have postulated as a source of material, there is no evidence that at this date any such existed. Whether any of the playhouse manuscripts provided by Heminge and Condell were in Shakespeare's autograph we can neither affirm nor deny, but it is well to be cautious in accepting at its face value the implication contained in their words that they had "scarce received from him a blot in his papers."

THE TITLE PAGE OF THE FIRST FOLIO
(*From the copy in the New York Public Library.*)

The First Folio is a large volume of 908 pages, measuring in the tallest extant copy 13¾ × 8½ inches. A reduced facsimile of the title page with the familiar wood-cut portrait appears on the opposite page. The text is printed in two columns with sixty-six lines to a column. The typography is only fairly good, and many mistakes occur in the pagination. Extant copies, of which there are nearly 200, vary in some respects, on account of the practice of making corrections while the sheets were being printed. The printer was William Jaggard, and his associates in the publishing enterprise were his son Isaac and the booksellers, William Aspley, John Smethwick, and Edward Blount. Estimates of the size of the edition vary from five to six hundred.

Many of the causes which made the text of these early editions inaccurate are common to all the plays, while some are peculiar to those obtained by reporters in the theater. Of the first, the most fundamental is, of course, the illegibility or ambiguity of the author's original manuscript. Such flaws were perpetuated and multiplied with each successive transcript, and when the manuscript copy came into the printer's hands, the errors of the compositor — confusion of words sounding alike, of words looking alike, unconscious substitution of synonyms, mere manual slips, and the like — were added to those already existing. The absence of any uniform spelling, and carelessness in punctuation, which led to these being freely modified by the printer, increased the risk of corruption. The punctuation of both Quartos and Folio, though by no means without weight, cannot be regarded as having the author's sanction, and all modernized editions re-punctuate with greater or less freedom. Most nineteenth-century editors carry on with minor modifications the punctuation of Pope, so that their texts show a composite of sixteenth, seventeenth, eighteenth, and nineteenth century methods; the text used in the Tudor edition is frankly punctuated, as far as the syntax permits, according to modern methods, with, it is believed, no loss in authority. There is no clear evidence that, in such productions as plays, proof was read outside of the printing-office. The theory, insisted on by Dr. Furness in successive volumes of the *New Variorum Shakespeare*, that the Elizabethan compositor set type to dictation is without foundation, the phenomena which he seeks to explain by it occurring commonly to-day when there is no question of such a practice.

Another class of variation in text arose from the treatment of the manuscript in the playhouse. Cuts, additions, and alterations were made for acting purposes, stage directions were added with or without the assistance of the author, revivals of the play called for revision by the original writer or another. The majority of stage directions in modern editions, except exits and entrances, are due to editors from Rowe onwards, and these unauthorized additions are distinguished in the Tudor edition by brackets. Almost all notes of place at the beginnings of scenes belong to this class.

The defects to which the texts of the surreptitiously obtained Quartos are particularly subject include omissions and alterations due to lapse of memory on the part of the actors, additions due to the tendency to improvise which Shakespeare censures in *Hamlet*, omissions due to the reporter's failure to hear or to write quickly enough, garbled paraphrases made up to supply such omissions, and the writing of prose as verse and verse as prose.

Such are the most important of the causes of the corruptions which the long series of editors of Shakespeare have devoted their study and their ingenuity to remedying. The series really begins with the second Folio of 1632 and is continued with but slight improvements in the third Folio of 1663, reprinted with the addition of *Pericles* and six spurious plays in 1664, and in the fourth Folio of 1685. The emendations made in the seventeenth-century editions are mainly modernizations in spelling and such minor changes as occurred to members of the printing staff. In no case do they have any authority except such as may be supposed to belong to a man not far removed from Shakespeare in date; and they add about as many mistakes as they remove.

The difficulty of the task of the modern editor varies greatly from play to play. It is least in the twenty plays for which the First Folio is the sole authority,

L

greater in the eight in which the Folio reprints a Quarto with some variations, greatest in the nine in which Folio and Quarto represent rival versions. In these last cases, it is the duty of the editor to decide from all the accessible data which version has the best claim to represent the author's intention, and to make that a basis to be departed from only in clear cases of corruption. The temptation, which no editor has completely resisted, is naturally towards an eclecticism which adopts the reading that seems most plausible in itself, without giving due weight to the general authority of the text chosen as a basis. If carried far, such eclecticism results in a patchwork quite distinct from any version that Shakespeare can have known.

The first editor of Shakespeare, in the modern sense, was Nicholas Rowe, poet laureate under Queen Anne. He published in 1709 an edition of the plays in six octavo volumes, preceded by the first formal memoir of the dramatist, and furnished with notes. The poems were issued in the following year in similar form, with essays by Gildon. Rowe based his text upon that of the fourth Folio, with hardly any collation of previous editions. He corrected a large number of the more obvious corruptions, the most notable of his emendations being perhaps the phrase in *Twelfth Night*, "Some are become great," which he changed to "Some are born great." On the external aspect of the plays Rowe has left a deeper mark than any subsequent editor. In the Folios only eight of the

plays had lists of *dramatis personæ;* Rowe supplied
them for the rest. In the Folios the division into
acts and scenes is carried out completely in only
seventeen cases, it is partially done in thirteen, and
in six it is not attempted at all. Rowe again completed the work, and though some of his divisions
have been modified and others should be, he performed
this task with care and intelligence. He modernized
the spelling and the punctuation, completed the exits
and entrances, corrected many corrupt speech-tags,
and arranged many passages where the verse was
disordered. In virtue of these services, he must, in
spite of his leaving much undone, be regarded as one
of the most important agents in the formation of our
modern text.

A second edition of Rowe's Shakespeare was published in 1714, and in 1725 appeared a splendid quarto
edition in six volumes, edited by Alexander Pope.
In his preface Pope made strong professions of his
good faith in dealing with the text. "I have dis-
charged," he said, "the dull duty of an editor to my
best judgment, with more labor than I expect thanks,
with a religious abhorrence of all innovation, and without
any indulgence to my private sense or conjecture. . . .
The various readings are fairly put in the margin, so
that anyone may compare 'em; and those I have preferred into the text are constantly *ex fide codicum,*
upon authority. . . . The more obsolete or unusual
words are explained." Hardly one of these state-

ments is entirely true. Pope possessed copies of the first and second Folios, and at least one Quarto of each play that had been printed before 1623, except *Much Ado*, but these he consulted only occasionally, and seldom registered the variants as he said he had done. When he did, he gave no clue to their source. He constantly inserted his private conjectures without notice, and his explanations of difficult expressions are few and frequently wrong. Passages considered by him inferior or spurious he relegated to the foot of the pages; others he merely omitted without notice. His ear was often jarred by the freedom of Shakespeare's verse, and he did his best to make it "regular" by eighteenth-century standards. Yet Pope spent much ingenuity in striving to better the text, and no small number of restorations and emendations are to be credited to him, especially in connection with the arrangement of the verse. He is to be credited also with discernment in rejecting the seven plays added to the Shakespearean canon in the third Folio, of which only *Pericles* has since been restored.

The weaknesses of Pope's edition did not long remain hidden. In the spring of 1726 appeared "Shakespeare Restored: or, a Specimen of the many Errors, as well committed, as unamended, by Mr. Pope in his late edition of this Poet. Designed not only to correct the said edition, but to restore the True Reading of Shakespeare in all the Editions ever yet publish'd." Lewis Theobald, the author, was a translator and scholar,

much better equipped than Pope for the work of edit-
ing, and his merciless exposure of Pope's defects gave
a foretaste of the critical ability later displayed in the
edition of Shakespeare which he published in 1734.
Lovers of Shakespeare discerned at the time the service
performed by Theobald in this attack on Pope, but the
publication in 1728 of the first edition of the *Dunciad*,
with Theobald as hero, gave Pope his revenge, and
cast over the reputation of his critic a cloud which is
only now dispersing. Modern scholarship, however,
has come to recognize the primacy of Theobald among
emendators of Shakespeare's text, and the most famous
of his contributions, his correction of "a table of green
fields" to "'a babled of green fields," in Quickly's
account of the death of Falstaff in *Henry V*, II. iii. 17,
is only a specially brilliant example of the combination
of acuteness, learning, and sympathy which made his
edition a landmark in the history of the text. For
many of his troubles, however, Theobald was himself
to blame; he attacked his opponents with unnecessary
vehemence, as he expressed his appreciation of his
own work with unnecessary emphasis; he was not
always candid as to what he owed to others, even to
the despised edition of Pope, from which he printed;
and he indulged his appetite for conjecture at times
beyond reasonable bounds.

Theobald's edition was followed in 1744 by that of
Sir Thomas Hanmer in six beautifully printed volumes.
This edition is based on that of Pope, and even goes

farther than Pope's in relegating to the foot of the page
passages supposed unworthy. Hanmer performed no
collating worth mentioning, but made some acute conjectures.

The student is apt to be prejudiced against the work
of William Warburton on account of the extravagance
of his claims and his ungenerous treatment of predecessors to whom he was greatly indebted. "The
Genuine Text," he announced, "(collated with all
former editions and then corrected and emended)
is here settled: Being restored from the Blunders of
the first editors and the Interpolations of the two
Last"; yet he based his text on Theobald's and joined
Pope's name with his own on the title-page. Whatever value belongs to Warburton's edition (1747) lies
in a number of probable conjectural emendations,
some of which he had previously allowed Theobald to
use, and in the amusing bombast and arrogance of many
of his notes. The feeble support that lay behind the
pretensions of this editor was exposed by a number
of critics such as John Upton, Zachary Grey, Benjamin
Heath, and Thomas Edwards, who did not issue new
editions, but contributed a considerable number of
corrections and interpretations.

The value of Dr. Johnson's edition (1765) does not lie
in his emendations, which are usually, though not
always, poor, or in his collation of older editions, for
which he was too indolent, but in the sturdy common-
sense of his interpretations and the consummate skill

frequently shown in paraphrases of obscure passages.
His Preface to the edition was the most weighty general estimate of Shakespeare so far produced, and
remains a valuable piece of criticism.   In scientific
treatment of the text, involving full use of all the
Quartos and Folios then accessible, Johnson and his
predecessors were far surpassed by Edward Capell, who
issued his edition in ten volumes in 1768.   Unfortu-
nately, the enormous labor Capell underwent did not
bear its full fruit, for he suppressed much of his textual
material in the interests of a well-printed page, and his
preface and notes are written in a crabbed style that
obscures the acuteness of his editorial intelligence.
He elaborated stage directions, and carried farther the
correction of disarranged meter; but, like most of his
fellow-editors in that century, he did less than justice
to his predecessors and was too indulgent to his own
conjectures.   This edition was supplemented by volumes of notes published in 1775 (1 vol.) and 1779–
1783 (3 vols.).

Before the publication of Capell's text, the antiquary George Steevens had issued in 1766 reprints of
twenty of the early Quartos; and in 1773 he produced,
in association with Johnson, an edition with a good text
in which he benefited from Capell's labors (though he
denies this).   Through his knowledge of Elizabethan literature he made substantial contributions to the interpretation of difficult passages.   He restored *Pericles* to
a place in the canon, but excluded the *Poems*, because

"the strongest Act of Parliament that could be framed
would fail to compel readers into their service." To
the second edition of Johnson and Steevens's text
(1778) Edmund Malone contributed his famous "Essay
on the Chronology of Shakespeare's Plays," which
began modern investigation of this subject. The
third edition was revised in 1785 by Isaac Reed; and
this was succeeded by the edition of Malone in 1790,
in which the vast learning and conscientious care of
that scholar combined to produce the most trustworthy text so far published. Malone was not brilliant, but he was extremely erudite and candid, and
his so-called "Third Variorum" edition in twenty-one
volumes, brought out after his death by James Boswell
in 1821, is a mine of information on theatrical history
and cognate matters, which will probably always be
of value to students of the period. The name of
"First Variorum Edition" is given to the fifth edition
of Johnson and Steevens, revised by Reed in 1803, and
"Second Variorum" to the sixth edition of the same,
1813. Meantime occasional critiques of complete
editions contributed something to the text. Johnson's
edition called forth comment by Kendrick in 1765
and Tyrwhitt in 1766, and the Johnson and Steevens
text was criticized by Joseph Ritson in 1783 and 1788,
and by J. Monck Mason in 1785. The first American
edition was published in Philadelphia in 1795–1796
from Johnson's text; the first continental edition at
Brunswick in 1797–1801 by C. Wagner.

The editions of the nineteenth century are too numerous for detailed mention here. Passing by the "family" Shakespeare of T. Bowdler, 1807 and 1820, and the editions of Harness, 1825, and Singer, 1826, we note the editions of 1838–1842, and 1842–1844 in which Charles Knight resorted to the text of the First Folio as an exclusive authority. J. P. Collier in his edition of 1844 leaned, on the other hand, to the side of the Quartos, but later became a clever if somewhat rash emendator, who spoiled his reputation by seeking to obtain authority for his guesses by forging them in a seventeenth-century hand in a copy of the second Folio. The colossal volumes of J. O. Halliwell-Phillipps's edition, 1853–1865, contain stores of antiquarian illustration; and in the edition of Delius, 1854–1861, we have the chief contribution of Germany to the text of Shakespeare. Delius, like Knight, though not to the same extreme, exaggerated the authority of the First Folio; but for the plays for which that is the sole source, his text has earned high respect. Alexander Dyce, wisest of Elizabethan scholars, produced in 1857 a characteristically sane text, on the whole the best to this date; while in America in 1857–1860 and 1859–1865 the brilliant but erratic Richard Grant White produced editions which show a commendable if puzzling openness to conviction in successive changes of opinion.

From 1863 to 1866 appeared the first issue of the Cambridge Shakespeare, edited originally by W. G.

Clark, J. Glover, and W. A. Wright. The responsibility
for the later revised edition of 1891–3 is Dr. Wright's.
The exceedingly careful and exhaustive collation of all
previous textual readings in the notes of this edition
make it indispensable for the serious student, and its
text, substantially reprinted in the Globe edition, is the
most widely accepted form of the works of Shakespeare
which has ever been circulated. The over-emphasis
on the First Folio which has been noted in Knight and
Delius is no longer found here, and in general the comparative value of Quarto and Folio is weighed in the
case of each play. Occasionally, in cases like that of
Richard III, where both Quarto and Folio are good
but vary widely, the Cambridge editors seem more
eclectic than their general theory warrants, and the
punctuation is still archaic, clinging to the eighteenth-
century tradition. But the acceptance of this careful
and conservative text has been a wholesome influence
in Shakespearean study.

The only completely reëdited texts which have
been issued since the revised Cambridge edition are
that of the Oxford Shakespeare, by W. J. Craig, on
principles very similar to the Cambridge, the Neilson
text, originally published in 1906 and revised and
reprinted in the Tudor Shakespeare, and that of the
new Cambridge edition, by Sir A. Quiller-Couch and
J. Dover Wilson. The New Variorum Shakespeare was
begun in 1871 by H. H. Furness and continued by his son,
H. H. Furness, Jr., up to the time of his death in 1930.

This monumental abstract of all previous criticism is of great value to the professional student of Shakespeare, and its textual apparatus has the advantage over the Cambridge edition of recording not only the first occurrence of a reading, but the names of the chief editors who have adopted it. It thus gives a compendious history of editorial judgment on all disputed points.

The conjectural emendation of Shakespeare still goes on, but since Dyce, comparatively few suggestions find general acceptance. In recent years the study of Elizabethan handwriting has received minute attention, and corrections suggested or supported by its observed peculiarities have received a considerable degree of approval. More progress has been made in interpretation through the greater accessibility of contemporary documents and the advance in recent years in our knowledge of Elizabethan theatrical conditions. But, in view of the circumstances under which the original editions were printed, there will always be room for variations of individual opinion in many cases, both as to what Shakespeare wrote and as to what he meant.

CHAPTER VIII

QUESTIONS OF AUTHENTICITY

OWING to the conditions of publication described in Chapter VII there are questions as to the authenticity of a number of the poems and plays ascribed to Shakespeare. Of the poems, " The Phœnix and the Turtle " and " A Lover's Complaint " have been sometimes rejected as unworthy, but there is no other evidence against the ascription to him by the original publishers. The case of *The Passionate Pilgrim* is different and is interesting as illustrating the methods of piracy practised by booksellers and as affording the only record of a protest by Shakespeare against the free use which they made of his name. This anthology was published by W. Jaggard in 1599 as " by W. Shakespeare." The third edition in 1612 added two pieces by Thomas Heywood. Heywood immediately protested and in the postscript to his *Apologie for Actors*, 1612, declared that Shakespeare was " much offended with M. Jaggard that (altogether unknown to him) presumed to make so bold with his name." Of the twenty poems that made up the volume, only five are certainly by Shakespeare, two appearing also in *The Sonnets* and three in *Love's Labour's Lost*. Six others can be assigned to contemporary poets. The authorship of the remaining nine is unknown, but probably only one or two are by Shakespeare.

In addition to the thirty-seven plays now included in all editions of Shakespeare, some forty others have been, for one reason or another, attributed to him. The First Folio contained thirty-six plays; and it is a strong evidence of the honesty and information of its editors, Heming and Condell, that subsequent criticism has been satisfied to retain the plays of their choice and to make but one addition, *Pericles*. Of these plays, however, it is now generally agreed that a number are not entirely the work of Shakespeare, but were written by him in part in collaboration with other writers, *e.g.*, *Titus Andronicus*, *1*, *2*, and *3 Henry VI*, *Timon of Athens*, *Pericles*, and *Henry VIII*. Of two of these, *Titus Andronicus* and *1 Henry VI*, some students refuse to give Shakespeare any share. Of the forty doubtful plays, there is not one which in its entirety is now credited to Shakespeare; and only three or four in which any number of competent critics see traces of his hand. Only in the case of *The Two Noble Kinsmen* is there any weight of evidence or opinion that he had a considerable share.

The second Folio kept to the thirty-six plays of the First Folio; but the second printing of the third Folio (1664) added seven plays: *Pericles Prince of Tyre*, *The London Prodigal*, *The History of Thomas Lord Cromwell*, *Sir John Oldcastle, Lord Cobham*, *The Puritan Widow*, *A Yorkshire Tragedy*, *The Tragedy of Locrine*.

These seven plays were also included in the fourth
Folio, and as supplementary volumes to Rowe's, Pope's,
and some later editions. They were all originally
published in quarto as by W. S., or William Shakespeare,
but except in the case of *Pericles*, this has been regarded
as a bookseller's mistake or deception without warrant.
Locrine, "newly set forth, overseen, and corrected
by W. S., 1595," is a play of about the date of *Titus
Andronicus*, and is probably by Greene, Peele, or some
imitator of Marlowe and Kyd. *Sir John Oldcastle*
appeared in 1600 in two quartos, one of which ascribed
it to William Shakespeare, but it was clearly composed for the Admiral's men as a rival to the Falstaff
plays which the Chamberlain's men had been acting.
Thomas Lord Cromwell (1602) and *The Puritan* (1607)
were ascribed to W. S., on their title-pages, but offer
no possible resemblances to Shakespeare. *The London
Prodigal* (1605) and *A Yorkshire Tragedy* (1608) were
both acted by Shakespeare's company, and bore his
name on their first editions, and the latter also on a
second edition, 1619. The external evidence for his
authorship is virtually the same as in the case of
Pericles, which also was acted by his company, appeared
under his name during his lifetime, but was rejected by
the editors of the First Folio. No one, however, can
discover any suggestion of Shakespeare in *The London
Prodigal*. *A Yorkshire Tragedy* is a domestic tragedy in
one act, dealing with a contemporary murder. It gives
the conclusion of a story also treated in a play, *The*

Miseries of Enforced Marriage (1607) by George Wilkins, the author of a novel *The Painful Adventures of Pericles*, and sometimes suggested as a collaborator on the play *Pericles*. *A Yorkshire Tragedy* is very unlike Shakespeare, but it has a few passages of extraordinarily vivid prose, which might conceivably owe something to him.

The Two Noble Kinsmen was registered April 8, 1634, and appeared in the same year with the following title-page "The Two Noble Kinsmen: Presented at the Blackfriars by the Kings Maiesties servants, with great applause: Written by the memorable Worthies of their time;

Mr. John Fletcher, and ⎱ Gent.
Mr. William Shakespeare ⎰

Printed at London by the Tho. Cotes for Iohn Waterson; and are to be sold at the signe of the Crowne in Paul's Church-yard. 1634." The exclusion of the play from the First Folio may be explained on the same basis as the exclusion of *Pericles;* for in each play Shakespeare wrote the minor part. There is now general agreement that *The Two Noble Kinsmen* was written by two authors with distinct styles, and that the author of the larger portion is Fletcher. The attribution of the non-Fletcherian part to Shakespeare has been upheld by Lamb, Coleridge, De Quincey, Spalding (in a notable Letter on Shakespeare's Authorship of *The Two Noble Kinsmen*, 1833), Furness, and Littledale (who edited the play for *The New Shakespeare*

Society, Series II, 1, 8, 15, London, 1876–1885) ; but
there are still many critics who do not believe that
Shakespeare had any part in the play. This question
will probably always remain a matter of opinion ;
but the evidence of various verse tests confirms esthetic
judgment in assigning about two fifths of the verse to
Shakespeare. The Shakespearean portion, here and
there possibly touched by Fletcher, includes, I. i ;
I. ii ; I. iii ; I. iv. 1–28 ; III. i ; III. ii ; V. i. 17–73 ; V. iii.
1–104 ; V. iv, and perhaps the prose II. i and IV. iii.

The dance in the play is borrowed from an anti-
masque in Beaumont's *Masque of the Inner Temple and
Gray's Inn*, presented at court, February 20, 1613. This
fixes the date of composition for the play in 1613, the
same year as *Henry VIII*, on which it is now generally
agreed that Shakespeare and Fletcher collaborated.
On both of the plays the collaboration seems to have
been direct ; *i.e.*, after making a fairly detailed outline,
each writer took certain scenes, and, to all intents,
completed these scenes after his own fashion.

One other play must be mentioned in connection
with *The Two Noble Kinsmen*. *Cardenio*, entered on
the Stationers' Register, 1653, was described as "by
Fletcher and Shakespeare." It seems probably identi-
cal with a *Cardenno* acted at court by the King's men
in May, 1613, and a *Cardenna* in June, 1613. Attempts
have been made to connect it with *Double Falsehood*,
assigned to Shakespeare by Theobald on its publication
in 1728.

Other non-extant plays ascribed to Shakespeare after 1642 require no attention, nor do a number of Elizabethan plays assigned to him in certain of their later quartos. Among these are *The Troublesome Reign of King John*, on which Shakespeare's *King John* was based; *The First Part of The Contention*, and (the Second Part) *The True Tragedy of Richard Duke of York* (versions of *2 Henry VI* and *3 Henry VI*); and *The Taming of a Shrew*, the basis of Shakespeare's play. The relation of Shakespeare's plays to these earlier versions is discussed in the introductions to the respective volumes of the Tudor Shakespeare. Other plays assigned, without grounds, to Shakespeare by late seventeenth-century booksellers are *The Merry Devil of Edmonton, The Arraignment of Paris, Fair Em, Mucedorus,* and *The Birth of Merlin*.

A few other anonymous plays have been ascribed to Shakespeare in whole or in part. Among these are *Arden of Feversham*, 1592, first attributed to Shakespeare by Edward Jacob in 1770; and *Edward III*, 1596, included with other false attributions to Shakespeare in a bookseller's list of 1659, and edited and assigned to Shakespeare by Capell in 1760. There is no evidence for the ascription of various portions of these plays to Shakespeare, except that certain passages seem to some critics characteristic of him. But at the date when the two plays were written his style had not attained its characteristic individuality; and the assignment of these anonymous plays to any particular

M

author neglects the obvious fact that many writers of that period present similar traits of versification and imagery. The attribution to Shakespeare of the Countess of Salisbury episode in *Edward III* and of a few passages in *Arden of Feversham* has scarcely any warrant beyond the enthusiastic admiration of certain critics for these passages.

In the case of the brief mob scene in the old play *Sir Thomas More*, Shakespeare's authorship, first suggested by Richard Simpson in 1871, has recently received support resting mainly on the theory that the handwriting of this scene of the manuscript is Shakespeare's. It would indeed be most interesting if we could recover a few pages from the poet's own pen, but detailed study seems to prove that the handwriting cannot be Shakespeare's. As to the passage itself, that is of little consequence; it is not beyond the reach of several other dramatists.

An account of the Shakespeare Apocrypha would be, however, incomplete without reference to a few of the many forgeries of documents or plays. John Jordan, a resident of Stratford, forged the will of Shakespeare's father, and probably some other papers in his *Collections*, 1780; William Henry Ireland, with the aid of his father, produced in 1796 a volume of forged papers purporting to relate to Shakespeare's career, and on April 2, 1796, Sheridan and Kemble presented at Drury Lane the tragedy of *Vortigern*, really by Ireland, but said by him to have been found among

Shakespeare's manuscripts. Ireland was exposed by Malone, and he published a confession of his forgeries in 1805. More skilful and far more disturbing to Shakespearean scholarship are the forgeries of John Payne Collier, extending over a period from 1831 to 1883. These included manuscript corrections in a copy of the second Folio, and many documents concerning the biography of Shakespeare and the history of the Elizabethan theater. These forgeries have vitiated all of Collier's most important publications, as his *Memoirs of Edward Alleyn*, and *History of English Dramatic Poetry*.

We turn now from attempts to increase Shakespeare's writings to an extraordinary effort to deny him the authorship of all his plays. Doubts on this score seem to have been raised by Joseph C. Hart in his *Romance of Yachting*, 1848, and by an article in *Chambers' Journal*, August 7, 1852. In 1856, Mr. W. H. Smith first proposed Bacon's authorship in a letter to Lord Ellesmere, "Was Lord Bacon the author of Shakespeare's plays?" These were followed by an article by Miss Delia Bacon in *Putnam's Monthly*, 1856, and a volume, *The Philosophy of the Plays of Shakespeare unfolded by Delia Bacon*. Since Miss Bacon's book, her hypothesis has resulted in the publication of hundreds of volumes and pamphlets supporting many variations of the theory. Some are content to view the authorship as a mystery, assigning the plays to an unknown author. Others attribute the author-

ship to a club of distinguished men, or to Sir Anthony
Shirley, or the Earl of Rutland, or another. Others
give Bacon only a portion of the plays, as those containing many legal terms. The majority, however,
are thoroughgoing "Baconians," and the most prodigious cases of misapplied ingenuity have been the
efforts to find in the First Folio a cipher, by which certain letters are selected which proclaim Bacon's authorship; as *The Great Cryptogram*, 1887, by Ignatius
Donnelly, and *The Bi-Literal Cypher of Francis Bacon*,
1900, by Mrs. Gallup. Such cyphers are mutually
destructive, and their absurdity has been repeatedly
demonstrated. Either they will not work without
much arbitrary manipulation, or they work too well and
are found to indicate Bacon's authorship of literature
written before his birth and after his death. Yet similar ' discoveries ' continue to be announced.

The evidences supporting Shakespeare's authorship
have been set forth sufficiently in this volume and
offer no basis for an attitude of skepticism. A few
considerations may be recalled as correctives for a
partial or mistaken reading of the evidence. (1)
Though the records of Shakespeare's life are meager,
they are fuller than for any other Elizabethan dramatist. Indeed we know little of the biography of any
men of the sixteenth century unless their lives affected
church or politics and hence found preservation in
the records. There is no 'mystery' about Shakespeare.
(2) Records amply establish the identity between

Shakespeare the actor and the writer. Moreover, the plays contain many words and phrases natural to an actor, many references to the actor's art, and show a wide and detailed knowledge of the ways and peculiarities of the theater. (3) The extent of observation and knowledge in the plays is, indeed, remarkable, but it is not accompanied by any indication of thorough scholarship, or a detailed connection with any profession outside of the theater, or a profound knowledge of the science or philosophy of the time. (4) The law terms are numerous, and usually correct, but do not establish any great knowledge of the law. Elizabethan London was full of law students who were among frequent patrons of the theater. Through acquaintance with these gentlemen Shakespeare might have readily acquired all the law that he displays. Moreover Shakespeare had an opportunity to gain a considerable familiarity with the law through the frequent litigations in which he and his father were concerned. (5) The dedication, commendatory poems, and address to the readers prefixed to the First Folio ought in themselves to be sufficient to remove the skepticism as to Shakespeare's authorship.

The following considerations apply to the attribution to Bacon, so far as that rests on any tangible basis: (1) Sir Tobie Matthews writes in a letter to Bacon, written some time later than January, 1621, "The most prodigious wit that ever I knew of my nation and of this side of the sea is of your Lordship's name, though he be known by another." The sentence probably refers to Father Thomas Southwell, a Jesuit, whose real surname was Bacon. There is nothing to connect it with Shakespeare. (2) The parallelisms between passages in Shakespeare and Bacon deal with phrases in common use and fail to establish any connection between the two men. (3) The few surviving examples of Bacon's verse suggest no ability as a poet. (4) Bacon's life is well known, and it offers no hint of connection with the theaters and no space in its crowded annals for the production of Shakespeare's plays. In fact, if we had to find an author for Shakespeare's plays among writers of the sixteenth and seventeenth centuries, Bacon would be about the last person conceivable.

CHAPTER IX

Shakespeare since 1616

During Shakespeare's lifetime, his plays were mentioned and imitated as often as those of any of his contemporaries. The more important documents bearing on his growing reputation have already been noted in this volume. This popularity, however, was confined to theater-goers and the readers of the sixteen plays that had appeared before 1616. There was no opportunity for a full estimate of his plays as literature until their publication in the Folio of 1623. This is given full and worthy expression in the fine verses which Ben Jonson contributed as a preface to the Folio. He had girded at several of Shakespeare's plays, and his own views of the principles and practices of the dramatic art were largely opposed to Shakespeare's, but he took this opportunity to express unstinted appreciation of Shakespeare's greatness. He notes with discrimination that Shakespeare learned his art in an earlier day, but far outshone Kyd, Lyly, and Marlowe.

> Soul of the Age
> The applause! delight! the wonder of our Stage!

He may challenge comparison with the great Greek tragedians, or in comedies

167

Of all that insolent Greece or haughty Rome
Sent forth, or since did from their ashes come.

He was not of an age but for all time !

The magnitude of Shakespeare's achievement was thus enthusiastically proclaimed by the literary dictator of the time.

From 1623, until the closing of the theaters, the plays continued favorites on the stage, though they yielded somewhat in the current taste to the theatrical successes of Fletcher and Massinger. After 1623, they continued to be read and admired, as is shown by the publication of the second and third folios in 1632 and 1663–1664, and by many appreciations, including those of D'Avenant, Suckling, the Duchess of Newcastle, and Milton. At the Restoration many of the plays were at once revived on the stage, and Dryden's essay *Of Dramatick Poesie* (1668) summed up in a masterly fashion contemporary opinion on Shakespeare. He is compared with other great dramatists, and is declared less correct than Jonson and less popular and modern than Beaumont and Fletcher, yet is "the man who of all Moderns, and perhaps Ancient Poets, had the largest and most comprehensive soul."

The Restoration was in some doubt about Shakespeare, for while it found in him much to admire, it also found much to condemn. His plays now had the advantage of women actors for the female parts, but

they encountered changed fashions in the theater. The
romantic comedies were not to the taste of the time, and
had little place on the stage until toward the middle of
the eighteenth century. Meanwhile, *The Merry Wives
of Windsor* was the most popular and most highly
esteemed of his comedies. The tragedies attracted the
genius of Betterton and were constantly acted, but these
were subject to revision of various kinds. *Hamlet* and
Othello held their places without alterations, but Nahum
Tate's tame version of *King Lear* and Cibber's version
of *Richard III* superseded the originals for many years.
Romeo and Juliet, too, gave way to Otway's *Caius
Marius*, 1692, which kept large portions of Shakespeare's play; and *Antony and Cleopatra* yielded place
on the stage to Dryden's fine *All for Love* (1678), in
the style of which he professes to imitate the "divine
Shakespeare." By 1692, adaptations had also been
made of *Troilus and Cressida*, *The Tempest*, *Macbeth*,
The Two Noble Kinsmen, *Timon*, *Richard II*, *Coriolanus*,
Henry VI, *Cymbeline*, *Titus Andronicus*, *Julius Cæsar*.
A great deal of contempt has been visited upon these
revisions of Shakespeare, and their attempts to improve on him are usually feeble enough; but sufficient
recognition has not been given to the testimony that
these revisors bear to a great appreciation and admiration of Shakespeare. They tried to adapt him to
current metrical conventions, to current literary
fashions, to an idea of art quite foreign to his, but
they made these efforts because they admired his

genius. If they did not admire everything in his thirty-seven plays, they admired a great deal.

Further, these revisions are the outcome of critical strictures on the plays which were then common and, in essence, have been frequently repeated. Critics objected to the irregularity and confusion of their structure, to their disregard of the unities of action, their mixture of tragic and comic, their obscurity and archaism of diction, their mixed and confused figures, their occasional puns and bombast. These are substantially the criticisms that Dryden offers when under the influence of Rymer. Rymer himself (*A Short View of Tragedy,* 1693) goes much farther. He desires tragedy to give a rationalized view of life, dealing poetic justice to various typical persons, and consequently condemns Shakespeare's persons as too individual, his plots as too irregular, and the total effect of his plays as insufficiently didactic and moral. This view of tragedy was mainly due to the rationalistic and classical ideas which continued for a century to dominate European criticism. But before the seventeenth century was over, Shakespeare's growing reputation had proved itself a rock against which the tendencies in criticism had broken like unavailing waves. However much they might insist on rules in art, critics were generally willing to hail Shakespeare as the great exception. Champions were ready to answer Rymer and to defend Shakespeare. *Othello,* selected by Rymer for special analysis and condemnation, continued to hold its place on the stage and to incite dramatists to emulation. The plays continued to be read, and new editions were demanded. In the forty years from 1660 to 1700, in spite of great changes in theatrical conditions, in spite of changes of taste in readers that relegated most of Elizabethan drama to neglect, and in spite of the formation of a criticism doubtful or neglectful of the very qualities in literature that his plays present, Shakespeare continued to win admirers. By 1700 he was recognized as a dramatist and poet who was one of the great possessions of the English race.

In the two centuries since, Shakespeare's fame and influence have spread and multiplied to an extent difficult to characterize justly in a brief summary. Some important evidences of this growth may indeed be collected and analyzed. The position and importance of his plays on the stage, the ever increasing number of editions, the changing attitudes of critics and men of letters — on these matters it is not difficult to draw conclusions as to Shakespeare's influence at home and abroad. But it is not so easy to say what his influence was on the literature of any generation, and still less easy to summarize with certainty the effects on thought and feeling and conduct which made up his continuing power over generation after generation of readers. This much is clear, that a study of Shakespeare's influence is in part a study of changing ideas and ideals in literature — that as he survived the Restoration taste, so he survived the new

classicism of the eighteenth and the romanticism of
the early nineteenth century. It is also clear that a
full record of the influence of Shakespeare on English-
speaking readers would touch on almost all the varied
changes of thought and conduct that have entered into
the history of two centuries.

The most important of the successive editions of
Shakespeare from that of Nicholas Rowe, 1709, to the
present time, have been noted in the history of the
text in Chapter VII. It must be observed that these
various publications indicate not only progress toward
establishing a sound text, but also a constantly increasing number of readers. The multiplication of editions
kept pace with the vast extension of the middle-class
interest in literature. By the end of the eighteenth
century, the works of Shakespeare were in the possession of everyone who had a library, and with a text
and notes that left few difficulties for a person of any
education.

The nineteenth century well maintained the tradition of earlier scholarship. Malone's extensive antiquarian knowledge of Elizabethan drama and theater
served as the basis for further research in these fields
by Dyce, Ward, Fleay, and others. The chronological
order of the plays, which Malone was the first to in-
vestigate, was determined with considerable certainty
and gave a new significance to the study of Shakespeare's work as a whole. Dyce, Sidney Walker, and
Wright, Delius of the Germans, Richard Grant White

of the Americans, are a few among the long list of
scholars who have added notable emendations and illustrative notes. Editions of the collected works indeed
soon became almost too numerous for record, and the
number of readings, notes, and illustrations too great
for collection even in the largest variorum. To-day
the task of scholarship may lie in the restriction, sim-
plification, and final determination of certain varying
editorial practices rather than in the accumulation of
further illustrative and appreciative comment. But
to the work of adding new editions there can be no
end so long as the number of readers increases. Volumes of all sizes, for many classes, following various
editorial methods, are likely to continue to meet the
changing but ever increasing demands of English-
speaking readers. At the end of the nineteenth century Shakespeare's works were not merely a household
possession, they were to be had in every possible form
to suit every possible taste or convenience.

The extension of Shakespeare's popularity on the
stage was concurrent with this widening range of
readers. In the first thirty years of the eighteenth
century, which marked a revolution in the nature of
the drama and the taste of the audiences, Shakespeare's
tragedies continued to be among the most frequently
acted stock plays at the two patented theaters. The
middle of the century saw the revival of most of the
romantic comedies and the appearance of David Garrick. Some of the adaptations continued, but others

were displaced by genuine Shakespeare, as in *Macbeth,
The Merchant of Venice*, and *Romeo and Juliet*. *All's
Well That Ends Well, As You Like It, Cymbeline, Much
Ado, Twelfth Night, The Winter's Tale*, were all revived.
In fact, if we include adaptations, every play of Shakespeare was seen on the stage during the eighteenth
century, with the exceptions of *2* and *3 Henry VI*, only
parts of these appearing, and of *Love's Labour's Lost*,
of which a version prepared for acting was published
in 1762 but not produced.

The traditions of Betterton had been carried on by
Wilks (1670–1732), Barton Booth (1681–1733), Colley
Cibber (1671–1757), and others. But the prevailing
manner was condemned as stiff and lifeless in comparison with the energy of Garrick's presentation.
From his first triumph in Richard III in 1741, to his
farewell performance of Lear in 1776, he won a series
of signal successes in both tragedy and comedy, in
Hamlet, Lear, Macbeth, Richard III, Falconbridge,
Romeo, Hotspur, Iago, Leontes, Posthumus, Benedick,
and Antony. Garrick's services to Shakespeare extended beyond the parts which he impersonated. He
revived many plays, and though he garbled the texts
freely, yet in comparison with earlier practice he really
had some right to boast that he had restored the text of
Shakespeare to the stage. Further, his example led
to an increased popularity of Shakespeare in the theater
and afforded new incentives for other actors. Mrs.
Clive, Mrs. Cibber, and Mrs. Pritchard were among

the women who acted with Garrick. Macklin, by his revival of Shylock as a tragic character, Henderson by his impersonation of Falstaff, and John Palmer in secondary characters, as Iago, Mercutio, Touchstone, and Sir Toby, were his contemporaries most famous in their day.

Garrick's place at the head of the English stage was taken by John Philip Kemble (1757–1823), an actor of great dignity of presence and manner, who won general admiration in the great tragic parts, especially those offering opportunities for declamation. His sister, Mrs. Sarah Siddons, was doubtless the greatest of English actresses; her Lady Macbeth, Queen Katherine, and Constance overwhelmed her audiences by their majesty and passion. Kemble's reputation was surpassed by Edmund Kean, whose appearance as Shylock in 1819, at Drury Lane, was the first of a series of great successes in most of the tragic parts, including Hamlet, Lear, Othello, and Richard III. In contrast to Kemble's declamation, Kean's acting was vehement and passionate. Coleridge declared that to see him was "reading Shakespeare by flashes of lightning." Readers of the dramatic criticism of Hazlitt and Lamb will recall tributes to Kean and to other favorite actors, especially perhaps their praise of Mrs. Jordan's Viola and Rosalind. Macready for forty years maintained the great traditions of English acting, and during his managements of Drury Lane sought to retain for Shakespeare's plays their preëminence on the

stage. Associated with his many impersonations were
those of Mrs. Warner and Helen Faucit (Lady Martin).
From Garrick's début to the retirement of Macready
(1851) is a century of great actors and actresses who
brought to the interpretation of the many characters
of the plays a skill and intelligence that satisfied the
most critical theater-goers and extended vastly the
appreciation and knowledge of Shakespeare's men and
women.

Shakespeare's position on the stage was, however,
maintained only with difficulty against the melodramas,
musical farces, and spectacles that absorbed the theaters.
Yet from 1844 to 1862, Samuel Phelps, at Sadler's
Wells, presented thirty-one of the plays. Since then
the stage has hardly seen an equally important revival;
but the great traditions of acting have been carried on
by many eminent actors: Sir Henry Irving, Ellen
Terry, Forbes Robertson, in England; Edwin Forrest,
Edwin Booth, Junius Brutus Booth, Walter Hampden,
Ada Rehan, Julia Marlowe, and Edward Sothern
in America. Lately, successful attempts have been
made to perform plays in the Elizabethan manner, and
perhaps there is a tendency to pay less attention to
elaborate scenic presentation than was the habit during
the last of the nineteenth century. In one respect, at
least, the present offers a decided improvement on the
past, for there is now a strong sentiment in favor of as
close an adherence as possible to an authorized text of
the plays.

Shakespeare has held his place on the stage in spite of many and great changes in theatrical conditions and dramatic taste. He will probably survive changes greater than those which separate the picture stage with its electric lights from the projecting open-air platform of his own day, or than those which separate the dramas of Ibsen, Shaw, and Barrie from those of Marlowe and Fletcher, or the cinematograph and comic opera from the bear-baiting and jugglery which rivaled the Globe. The visitor who scans, in the Stratford Museum, the curious collection of portraits of actors and actresses in Shakespearean parts may wonder what peculiarities of costume, manner, and expression will be devised for the admired interpretations of the centuries to come. But it hardly seems possible that any actor of the future will influence as greatly the appreciation of Shakespeare's characters and speeches as did Garrick and Mrs. Siddons in England or Edwin Booth in America.

Shakespearean criticism in the eighteenth century was, as has been noted, largely textual, but there was also a considerable discussion of Shakespeare's learning, his art, and its violations of neo-classical theory. John Dennis, in his *Letters*, 1711, proved a sturdy admirer, and the consensus of opinion of following writers was that of Sedley's couplet which described Shakespeare as

> The pride of Nature, and the shame of Schools,
> Born to Create, and not to Learn from Rules.

N

Voltaire's attacks brought rejoinders from Mrs. Elizabeth Montagu in 1769 and from Dr. Johnson in the preface to his edition, 1765. In fact, admiration for Shakespeare was a powerful factor in forcing the rejection of rules and standards of French criticism. Johnson's Preface finds fault with Shakespeare's neglect of poetic justice and dwells at length on the faults in plots and diction, but Johnson defends the violation of the unities, and his praise is a discriminating summary of the merits that the eighteenth century had found in Shakespeare. It is praise that is likely to endure.

Within another generation, however, reverence for Shakespeare had increased to an intensity that made Johnson's admiration seem feeble and niggardly. This transformation was due to many causes, but in the main it was a part of the vast changes in European literature known as the Romantic movement. This resulted in a rejection of the rules and models of neo-classicism, a new interest in the literature and manners of the Middle Ages, a conception of poetry as the expression of individuality, attention to the individual man in all orders of society, a fresh concern for external nature, an emphasis on the emotions rather than mere reason, a desire for wonder and mystery, and an exaltation of natural instincts and intuitions as opposed to general truths or social conventions. In each of these particulars, Shakespeare seemed the complete fulfilment of the new tendencies — which indeed his growing influence had undoubtedly encouraged. More than Spenser or

Milton or the old ballads, he was the inspiration and guide for new endeavors in literature. It seemed to the new age of critics and poets that they had redis- covered him, and they hastened to raise him from neg- lect to the throne of omniscience. He was no longer a wayward genius, he was the model from whom art and wisdom were to be learned.

This new criticism was esthetic and appreciative. It did not try to balance Shakespeare's merits and faults, or to test him by codes of arts or morals. It recognized him as supreme, and its discipleship was devoted to reverent interpretation and enthusiastic admiration. Believing in the importance of the poetic imagination in the affairs of men, it found in him a gospel and an example for its creed. Its delightful task was to find new beauties and to search out the hiding-places that revealed the god of its idolatry. If the genius of the master-poet was the source of art and wisdom, the personality of the critic gained a new refulgence through its service of reflecting the rays of glory. The interest in the study of individual charac- ters had resulted, even in Johnson's day, in some not- able interpretive essays, as Maurice Morgann's on Falstaff (1777). In the next generation, Coleridge, Lamb, and Hazlitt in England, and Schlegel and Goethe in Germany, brought the keenest intelligence and most sympathetic taste to a criticism that aspired to reveal the full range and height of Shakespeare's creative faculty.

The results of this criticism may be more specifically summarized. (1) It viewed the individual characters of the plays as if they were real persons, analyzing their motives and elaborating or repainting their portraits, as in the analyses of Hamlet by Goethe and Coleridge, or in the brilliant sketches of Hazlitt. The few hundred lines spoken by a leading character have thus been expanded by the impressions made on successive critics into volumes of biography. (2) Shakespeare's works were studied as a whole in an effort to study the development of his art and mind. Schlegel and Coleridge gave a unity to the phenomena of the thirty-seven plays that had not been recognized hitherto; but they and their followers naturally tended to make of their author a sort of nineteenth-century romanticist. (3) Exalting the services of poetry and the creative imagination, they viewed Shakespeare's exhibition of human nature and his incidental wisdom as profound, consistent, and immensely valuable for the human race. Hence they were ever seeking in his work for a philosophy, a synthetic ethics, and making the widest applications of his words to conduct. Believing that he could do no wrong, they inevitably came to attribute to him ideas and morals that were of their own creation.

The defects of this criticism are most apparent in critics like Ulrici and Gervinus who carry its methods to extremes. Personal, fanciful, unhistorical, idolatrous, it is yet a tremendous tribute and an amazing record of the sway that Shakespeare has exerted on the human mind. The writings of no other man have been studied so intimately by so many sympathetic readers, or have excited such different impressions. Throughout the nineteenth century this appreciative criticism has continued, and Shakespeare has been interpreted through the personality of many critics, German and American, as well as British, more recently through the delicate sensibility of Professor Dowden, and the penetrating reflection of Professor A. C. Bradley.

At the end of the nineteenth century, Shakespearean criticism has become too varied for a brief survey. Textual and esthetic criticism both continue. The biography has been established on a sound basis of fact by Halliwell-Phillipps and Sidney Lee; and still new facts reward patient investigators of the legal and court documents, almost the only records preserved that can possibly bear on Shakespeare's life. Special studies of all sorts have been numerous, as to his reading, religion, folk-lore, and so on. More significant in its effect on our general view have been the efforts of historical criticism. As our knowledge of Elizabethan literature, drama, theater, have increased, it has been possible to see Shakespeare in relation to his time and environment. The study of Shakespeare as a sixteenth-century dramatist aims not merely at a better appreciation of his work, but also to explain his development and to account for some of the qualities of his achievement. Its attitude is that of the scientific historian examining the records of any great human activity, and trying to understand its causes, results, and meaning. Somewhat allied to this has been technical dramatic criticism, which is uniting knowledge of the Elizabethan theater with interest in drama as a peculiar form, and thereby studying Shakespeare as a dramatist rather than as a poet or philosopher. In fact, Shakespeare is no longer merely man, poet, dramatist, philosopher, or genius. Jonson's tribute, Dryden's summary, Johnson's judicial essay, or Coleridge's admiring studies, all seem hopelessly inadequate to express the range of his dominion. He has become the source of the most various and extensive interests, a continent that ever expands its fields for exploration, an epoch that ever extends the years of its duration, a race that never dies, though its progeny ever multiplies.

It is in the nineteenth century that Shakespeare's dominance becomes international. Four of his plays were acted at Dresden and elsewhere early in the seventeenth century, but there seems to have been no literary acquaintance with the plays in Germany until about the middle of the eighteenth century, when two poor translations of *Julius Cæsar* and *Romeo and Juliet* appeared, and J. C. Gottsched severely criticized Shakespeare's art. In 1759, in a journal, "Litteraturbriefe," Lessing began a warm defense of Shakespeare and declared his superiority to Racine and Corneille. His *Hamburgische Dramaturgie* (1767) went far in directing the change of taste from French clas-

sicism and in establishing Shakespeare in German
thought as the greatest of poets, whether ancient or
modern.   A prose translation was begun by Wieland
in 1762 and completed by Eschenburg in 1789.   What
is perhaps the best translation of Shakespeare into
any foreign tongue was begun in 1797 by A. W. von
Schlegel and Ludwig Tieck, two leaders of German
romanticism, and finally completed in 1853.   Schlegel's
lectures on *Shakespeare and the Drama* were delivered
in Vienna in 1808, and present both the romanticist's
idolizing of Shakespeare and a new kind of esthetic
criticism destined to exercise great influence on Coleridge and the English critics.   Meanwhile Goethe was
adapting *Romeo and Juliet* for the Weimar theater
(1801) and Schiller was arranging *Macbeth* for presentation at Stuttgart (1801).   Goethe indeed was, throughout his life, an enthusiastic admirer of Shakespeare, and
his works are full of discriminating criticism, of which
perhaps the most famous passage is the analysis of
Hamlet in *Wilhelm Meister*.   Since Lessing and Her-
der, German poetry and drama have felt Shakespeare's
influence, and in both textual and esthetic criticism,
Germany has rivaled England and the United States.
Delius and Schmidt, whose *Shakespeare-Lexicon* (1874)
is one of the great monuments of Shakespeare scholarship, are perhaps first among textual students; since
1865 the German Shakespeare Society has published
yearly contributions of all kinds to Shakespeare criticism, and especially an excellent bibliography.   On the

stage Shakespeare has been constantly acted since the beginning of the century, and has engaged the services of some of the greatest actors, as Schroeder, the two Devrients, and Barnay. At present a large number of his plays are performed annually, in the smaller as well as the larger cities, and more frequently than in Britain or America. Twenty-six of the plays were acted in 1911, *Othello* leading with 158 performances. For the years 1909, 1910, 1911, *Hamlet, Othello, The Merchant of Venice* have been the favorites, with *The Taming of the Shrew* and *A Midsummer-Night's Dream* the most popular of the comedies. For over a century Shakespeare has profoundly influenced German life and letters. Rarely, if ever, has a great people been so powerfully affected by a writer in a foreign tongue.

In France, during the eighteenth century, Shakespeare's reputation was both aided and hindered by Voltaire. Though there are a few earlier notices of the English dramatist, Voltaire, after his visit to England, 1720–1729, was virtually the first to win attention for Shakespeare. He admired Shakespeare, acknowledged his influence, but deplored his deficiencies in taste and art, "le Corneille de Londres, grand fou d'ailleurs, mais il a des morceaux admirables." Voltaire's criticism provoked replies in England and a defense from Diderot, who shared with Lessing the effort to emancipate the drama from some of its neoclassical restriction. Translations of twelve plays by La Place (1745–1748) and all of the plays by Le Tourneur (1776–1782) gave an opportunity for greater acquaintance with his work. A version of *Hamlet* by Ducis was acted at Paris in 1769. But even at the end of the century, French literary opinion, though partly won by Le Tourneur's praise of Shakespeare, still sympathized with Voltaire, now engaged in an attack on Englishmen and their favorite. His last opinion (1778) declares, "Shakespeare est un sauvage avec des étincelles de génie qui brillent dans une nuit horrible."

The nineteenth century saw a reaction from this criticism, indicated by the praise of Madame de Staël (*De la Litterature*, 1804), by Guizot's essay accompanying a revision of Le Tourneur's translation (1821), and later in the appreciation of Mézières's *Shakespeare ses Œuvres et ses Critiques* (1860), in several translations, and in Victor Hugo's eulogy (1869). The best of the translations is by the poet's son, François Victor Hugo in prose (1859–1866). On the Paris stage, the leading English actors have appeared from time to time, and French versions of *Hamlet*, *Macbeth*, and *Othello* have made a permanent place. M. Jusserand is the chief authority for the history of Shakespeare in France and an ambassador of peace between the conflicting literary tastes of the two nations.

In Italy, Holland, Russia, Poland, and Hungary, during the nineteenth century, many of the plays have been regularly acted, and from Italy have come great actors and actresses, as Ristori, Salvini, and Rossi.

Complete translations have been published in these countries and in Bohemian, Swedish, Danish, Finnish, and Spanish; and separate plays have been translated and acted in many other languages including those of India, Japan, and China.

In music and painting Shakespeare's influence has also been international. Books have been devoted to the history of Shakespeare's music, and such surveys include nearly every English composer of note, and also Schubert, Schumann, Mendelssohn, Berlioz, Ambroise Thomas, Saint Saëns, Rossini, and Verdi. In painting as well, the persons and scenes of the play have excited the efforts of English, German, and American artists.

In America, as has already been indicated, the interest in Shakespeare is hardly separable from that in Great Britain. Editors, critics, scholars, have been numerous and their contributions important, and the plays have been acted constantly and widely through the country. Probably there is no part of the world to-day where the study of Shakespeare is so active and where the interest in his work is so widespread. In one respect, at least, the United States in recent years has carried this study and interest beyond England, in the fields of education. As the study of the mother tongue has become the basis of American education, so Shakespeare has come to play a more and more important part in the training of youth. The universities offer training in the various departments of Shakespearean

scholarship, every college offers courses on his plays, a
number of them are prescribed for reading and study
in the high schools; a few of them are read and ex-
tracts memorized in the primary schools. The child
begins his education with Ariel and the fairies, and
until his schooling is completed is kept in almost daily
intercourse with the poetry and persons of the dramas.
Homer was not better known in Athens. In a democracy still young and widely separated from older
nations and cultures, Shakespeare has become one of
the links that bind the American public not only to
the common inheritances of the English-speaking races,
but to the traditional culture of Europe.

Known in the literature and theater of every civilized
nation, the subject of a vast and increasing amount of
discussion and criticism, the source of a scholarship
rivaling that devoted to the writers of antiquity, the
familiar theme for music and painting, the household
possession of Great Britain, Germany, and America,
influencing thought and conduct as few books have
ever influenced them, and now an important element
in the education of a great democracy, — the plays of
Shakespeare occupy a position whence imagination
"can not pierce a wink beyond, but doubt discovery
there." His reputation and influence must change
greatly in the years to come; but this at least is secure
— three hundred years of an ever increasing sway over
the human mind.

CHAPTER X

Conclusion

THE purpose of this volume has been to summarize what we know about Shakespeare. The documentary records and early traditions of his life have been supplemented by information in regard to the times and places in which he lived, the literature which he read, and the theaters for which he worked. The evolution of the drama that grew up in those theaters has been reviewed, and its manifest connections with Shakespeare's own development have been indicated. That development has been traced by means of a careful determination of the chronology of the plays; and the recognition of this growth of his powers has been shown to be a necessary basis for a just estimate of their achievement.

If, now, in conclusion, we attempt to define our general impression of the man and his work, this must inevitably take into account considerations of environment and development. The man belonged to his era, his city, and his profession. The documents make it plain that he did not live apart, but in close contact with the affairs of his day and generation. The plays make it clear that few men ever became so intimately familiar with the manners, morals, and ideas of their own time. There is no doubt that he drank deeply of the experience that Elizabethan London offered him. Still more, the plays make it clear that his life was one of constant and extraordinary intellectual and spiritual growth. Though, from the objective nature of the dramas, it is impossible to translate them into terms of personal experience or into exact stages of mental growth, yet it is none the less evident that the progress from the author of *Love's Labour's Lost* to the author of *The Tempest*, from the creator of Richard III and Valentine to the creator of Iago and Antony, was marked, not only by a widening experience, but also by a development of personal character.

To understand a man's surroundings does not, however, reveal the man; and to measure the growth of genius does not interpret its quality. Lovers of the plays are likely always to query: What manner of man was this? Taken out of his London, at any time in his career, how would he seem if we could know him as a man? Of what nature is this companion and friend whose presence we have felt through all his verses and in all of his characters? The few clues offered by records or tradition, and the difficulties in separating the creator from the thousand men and women of his creation, have driven many to seek answers to these questions in the sonnets. There he speaks in the first person, and there are revealed not merely some dubious hints of actual incidents, but

the surer indications of emotional conflicts that went
to the heart of the man's nature. At their worst,
the sonnets may have been only literary exercises on
conventional themes, but at their best they are surely
both superb poetry and the result of genuine emotion.
Can we doubt that the poet knew the pitfalls that
beset the course of human passion or that he had
faith in the triumphant beauty of love and friendship?
Yet the most splendid of these lyrical declarations of
faith add little to what we knew of the creator of the
lovers and friends of the dramas. The trivialities and
the sublimities, the sin and the idealism of the sonnets
coalesce with the emotional effects of the comedies and
tragedies. In forming our impression of the man,
whatever we may derive from the sonnets does not
contradict and does not largely affect the impressions
made by the poetry and humanity of the plays. For
the conception which each one forms of Shakespeare
the man must be derived in the main from the impressions of personality implied by the plays. Such a
conception is bound to be individual and without
validity that can rest on proofs, but in the main it
has not varied greatly from individual to individual
or from generation to generation. From Jonson and
Dryden to Goethe and Tennyson, there has been no
great difference in the essentials of this estimate of
the man.

If the plays do not throw a clear light on matters
of conduct and exercise of the will, they certainly tell

of no lack of self-control and no weakness or feverishness of action. The traditions of conviviality and the records of a life of constant industry that secured wealth and social position are both in accord with the impressions derived from the plays of an eagerness for experience controlled by a self-mastery and a serenity of purpose. If one were to search for a modern writer most like Shakespeare, one would select Scott, rather than Shelley, or Byron, or Wordsworth. As to the intellectual quality of the author of the plays, it is clear that he was not a Galileo or a Bacon. If we judge intellectual power by its creation of system or synthesis, we shall probably estimate Shakespeare less highly than if we remember that intellect of the highest order is often displayed by maintaining openness and largeness of view in face of the solicitations of theory or prejudice. No one can read the plays in connection with the literature of the time, or of any time, without marveling at their freedom from vulgarity, pettiness, or narrowness of mental attitude. If they do not afford evidences of a profound culture in philosophy, letters, or science, they offer no trace of intellectual blindness or conceit, and they leave no doubt that their author had thought greatly and freely. Even more certain is their assurance of the range and intensity of his emotional life. In these respects again, no one can compare his work with that of other writers without feeling the effect of his personality. Fletcher, perhaps next to him among the Elizabethans in a

versatile expression of a wide range of emotions, gives
no sign of the sincere, profound, and searching interest
in humankind which we are sure was Shakespeare's.
Bacon, surpassing him perhaps in intellectual curiosity
and thoroughness, manifestly gives no evidence in
his writings of the warmth of sympathy, the quickness
of emotional response, the fire of passion which we find
in the author of Shakespeare's plays. It is difficult
to disbelieve that their imaginative participation in the
height and breadth of human feeling was the creation
of a man who united intellectual greatness with an
emotional susceptibility of extraordinary range and
delicacy, and with a sympathy, genial, wide, tolerant,
but also heartfelt, deep, and passionate. Such is
the ineffaceable impression of the man which has been
shared by many generations of readers, and which
found expression two hundred and fifty years ago in
Dryden's carefully considered estimate, "The man who
of all Moderns, and perhaps Ancient Poets, had the
largest and most comprehensive soul."

What of the plays themselves? Is there any fixed
and universal estimate of their quality and significance
as literature? In this volume we have been concerned
in reviewing our knowledge about them rather than
in their interpretation or evaluation. We have noted
the sources from which their plots were drawn, the
conditions under which they were produced in the playhouses, the influences at work in the contemporary
drama which determined in some measure their sub-

jects and treatment. Starting with the probable
dates of their composition, we have traced them from
the theater to the printer, through the hands of
many editors, and through the long history of their
effects on theatergoers and readers. In their history
they have played a part in the changes of taste and opinion of three centuries, and if they have grown greatly in
men's estimation, this has not been without much vari-
ability of appreciation and uncertainty as to their value.
What, then, are the qualities of the plays that raised
them at once above the measure of contemporary
influence and rivalry? Are these the qualities that
have continued to win the most general appreciation?
Despite all the stress we are to-day taught to place
on change, growth, evolution, are there qualities
in these plays which insure them a continued pre-
eminence in literature?

Differences of opinion testify, indeed, to the comprehensive appeal of the plays to different minds, nations,
or epochs, but they have not greatly affected the
essential elements in men's admiration. If some critic
brings into new prominence a quality that has partly
escaped attention, his discovery is not likely to affect
the more permanent elements of their reputation. If
for a time attention is turned to the plays as plays
rather than as poems and to the merits of Shakespeare
as a dramatist, this criticism does not lead to any
lasting disregard of their poetic quality or to the permanent acceptance of skill in dramatic structure

o

as a chief element in their literary preëminence. Nor is such an element discoverable in their philosophical synthesis or their incidental wisdom, although some of the most brilliant criticism has exalted that wisdom or sought to formulate and expound their view of life. Concerning the essential elements of their greatness no real difference of opinion has arisen from the time they were written down to the present day. They were lifted at once above the level of contemporary endeavor, and they have continued to grow in reputation chiefly because of their poetry and their characterization.

Concerning the nature and quality of these there is little difference of opinion, though critics may vary in estimating their beauty or value. One may prefer the verse of Homer or of Milton, but he will not deny the traits that distinguish Shakespeare's. Another may prefer the well-ordered study of human motives in Sophocles, or the realistic analysis of a modern realist like Turgenieff, but he will recognize the qualities in Shakespeare's characterization that are the basis of general admiration. Still another may condemn that admiration, but he will not differ from us as to the chief sources of its existence.

These two sources are hardly to be separated, for the persons are revealed through the beauty of the verse, and the poetry is ever adapted to the speakers. In the early plays the poet's fancy often refuses to be bound by the requirements of his characters and escapes in lyric or descriptive excursions; but as his art becomes more masterly, the poetry adapts itself with increasing devotion to the dramatic task, discarding the limitations of the verse form and even at times sacrificing clarity and harmony of expression in its effort to make a few lines significant of the thought and emotion of some individual. An enormous vocabulary is treated with daring freedom; words are coined, changed, or restamped in order to let nothing of significance escape. The effect is not primarily that of finished workmanship or elaborate harmony, though these may be found in many passages and notably in the greatest of the sonnets. Broken rather than completed images, richness of suggestion rather than unity of impressiveness, surprise and novelty in words rather than their delicate adjustment, make up an effect of bewildering enchantment rather than of perfected form. This is true even in an early play like *Romeo and Juliet*, where the verse becomes undramatic in order to make the most of every opportunity for fancy or melody, and it is true also in *Othello*, where poetry and characterization are wedded with consummate art. The reader's pleasure is not in finding each idea finally developed or each motive given full elaboration. It is rather in the flow of words which endow each person and moment with their wealth of color and suggestion, and somehow carry on to the reader both their impression of life and the transforming power of their dignity and splendor.

In a last analysis the quality of the poetry is less

dependent on the music of line or passage than on the imagery of the words themselves. It seems as if the imagination had hurried on Ariel's wing around the universe in order to freight each phrase with a fresh trope and an unexpected meaning. Sometimes, to be sure, there results an excess or mixture of figures; but restrained to character and situation, bound by the measure of the pentameter, the carnival of words becomes a gorgeous yet ordered pageant, the very spectacle of beauty.

Let us take but one passage, not from the great crises of passion, nor from those unsurpassable revelations of the tortured spirit, but from the opening of a play where the purpose is chiefly expository, and where indeed the language is not free from that mixture of figures which some condemn. The wonderful first scene of *Antony and Cleopatra*, which within the compass of its sixty-two lines presents the two protagonists and their background of empire and war, opens thus in the speech of a subordinate.

> Nay, but this dotage of our general's
> O'erflows the measure. Those his goodly eyes,
> That o'er the files and musters of the war
> Have glow'd like plated Mars, now bend, now turn
> The office and devotion of their view
> Upon a tawny front; his captain's heart,
> Which in the scuffles of great fights hath burst
> The buckles on his breast, reneges all temper,
> And is become the bellows and the fan
> To cool a gipsy's lust.

A few lines further on Antony speaks thus, as he embraces Cleopatra.

> Let Rome in Tiber melt, and the wide arch
> Of the rang'd Empire fall! Here is my space.
> Kingdoms are clay; our dungy earth alike
> Feeds beast as man; the nobleness of life
> Is to do thus, when such a mutual pair
> And such a twain can do't, in which I bind,
> On pain of punishment, the world to wit
> We stand up peerless.

No other man ever wrote verse like this; and it is hard to believe that words will ever again respond to such a magician.

This poetry is the fitting accompaniment of a characterization, the range and vitality of which, the world to wit, stand up peerless. While these are in general qualities of the Elizabethan drama, it is noteworthy that almost from the beginning Shakespeare outstripped his rivals. Launce, Richard III, Shylock, Juliet, were enough to establish a supremacy. The years that followed with their maturing thought and experience gave an amazing development to what was manifestly the native bent of his genius. Whatever else one may find in the plays, indeed whatever one finds there of wisdom or beauty, truth or art, it cannot be separated from their revelation of human nature.

It is this primarily that makes the dramas great and lasting. The histories, with all their pomp and movement and patriotism, reveal kings and lords and peasants as alike the subjects of changing fortune, alike human beings for our pity, admiration, or laughter. The comedies with their fancy and sentiment and fun, and their perennial sunshine on the self-deceived and selfish, are ruled by the most charming and refined of womankind. The tragedies with their presentation of the waste and suffering of life, though here depravity may seem to fill the scene and innocence share in the punishment and ruin, yet redeem us from the terror of their devastation by their assurances of both the majesty and the loveliness of men and women.

Shakespeare's methods in characterization have seemed to some haphazard and bewildering. He does not fit his men and women into an analysis of the constitution of society or into an obvious view of man's relations in the universe. Nor does he use his characters to illustrate fixed conceptions or processes of cause and effect. He usually started with an old story, with certain types of character, and he was not forgetful of theatrical necessities or dramatic construction. But as he went on he brought all his astounding interest in human nature to focus on the old plot and the stock type. Hamlet, the hesitating avenger, becomes the sentimentalist, the idealist, the thinker at war with himself, the embodiment of that conflict between circumstance and a nature unfitted to its task, which in some measure we have all encountered in life. An arrogant and doting old man, by the force of creative imagination, transcends the nursery tale from which he came, and

carries to us all the implications of suffering and love
that surround the aging of parents and the growth of
children. Cleopatra is a wanton, but no analysis
can explain the subtleties with which the idealism and
animalism, the sacrifice and frivolity — and how much
else — of human passion are bound together in the few
hundred lines which she speaks. It is impossible to
affirm that each of the great characters is thoroughly
consistent or offers a strictly accurate motivation.
Rather, they are magnificent portraits — like the
Mona Lisa — crowded with a penetrating but question-
provoking psychology. Into such parts and situations
as the drama could afford are impressed every
possible revelation of our motives; but his model was
always reality and he never yielded truth to whim or
prepossession.

Human nature, at its best or worst, droll or tragic,
is thus given magnitude and potency. This idealization,
rendered still more effective by the verse, persuades
us as we read that here are our own attributes and
conflicts exalted, now into serene beauty, again
into torment and horror, and again into the Olympic
warfare of unknown supermen. No doubt there is
confusion because of the complexity of motives depicted
and the multiplicity of impressions created, but there
is also a final message of the greatness and comprehen-
siveness of human souls. In this world of sin and
weakness and death, it is human beings, however
mocked or maltreated by circumstance or by them-

selves, that are still triumphant and interesting. Out of his strifes and failures, the individual man yet emerges, the object of our contemplation and the assurance of our faith.

In periods or persons when interest in the individual gives way to thought about class or system or some form of organization, it is likely that admiration for Shakespeare's plays will suffer a decline. In periods or persons when the individual assumes a larger place in thought and his power to affect and dominate the world is emphasized, the plays are likely to acquire a new regard. As long, however, as the study of human nature is a chief occupation of mankind and as long as we believe that a great purpose of imaginative litera- ture is to enlarge our knowledge and sympathy for our fellows, so long, we may be sure, these dramas will not lose their preëminence in literature.

APPENDICES

Appendix A

I. REPOSITORIES OF DOCUMENTS

L. refers to Lambert's *Shakespeare Documents* and H.-P. to Halliwell-Phillipps's *Outlines of the Life of Shakespeare.* 7th ed.

1

THE PARISH REGISTERS OF STRATFORD-ON-AVON are the authority for the baptisms of John Shakespeare's seven children (L. 1–7); for the burials of Anne and Edmund (L. 10); for the baptisms of William Shakespeare's daughter Susanna (L. 13) and the twins, Hamnet and Judith (L. 14); for the burials of Hamnet (L. 28), of the poet's father, John (L. 75), of his mother, Mary (L. 110), of the poet himself (L. 146), and of his widow (L. 159). These Registers have been edited for the Parish Registers Society, by R. Savage, 1898–9.

2

THE CORPORATION RECORDS OF STRATFORD-ON-AVON contain the Quiney-Sturley correspondence (L. 39, 43, 44; H.-P. II. 57–60); a return of the quantities of corn and malt held by the inhabitants of the ward in which New Place was situated, "Wm. Shackespere" being down for ten quarters (L. 53); a Bill of Complaint presented by R. Lane, T. Green, and William Shakespeare respecting the tithes of Stratford-upon-

Avon (L. 125); the answer of William Combe to the foregoing Bill (L. 126).

3

THE PUBLIC RECORD OFFICE IN LONDON preserves the following: record of the purchase by John Shakespeare of two
houses on Henley Street, Stratford-on-Avon (L. 8); record
of a mortgage on an estate at "Awston Cawntlett" given to
Edmund Lambert by John and Mary Shakespeare (L. 9);
Bill of Complaint brought by John Shakespeare against John,
son of Edmund Lambert, respecting an estate at Wilmecote,
near Stratford (L. 15); Ms. accounts of the Treasurer of the
Chamber, "To Willm. Kempe, Willm. Shakespeare &
Richarde Burbage, servaunts to the Lord Chamberleyne, upon
the Councelles warrant dated at Whitehall xv^{to} Marcij 1594
for twoe severall Comedies or enterludes shewed by them
before her Majestie in Christmas tyme laste paste, viz: upon
St. Stephens daye and Innocentes daye xiij.li. vj.s. viijd.,
and by waye of her Majesties rewarde vj.li. xiii.s. iiijd. in all
xx.li." (L. 25); record of the purchase of New Place by Shakespeare (L. 32); papers in a Chancery suit relating to the
estate at Wilmecote mortgaged to Edmund Lambert, and
consisting of a Bill of Complaint by John and Mary Shakespeare against John Lambert for his refusal to accept £40
and reconvey the property to the complainants, John Lambert's answer, and the replication of John and Mary Shakespeare to the answer (L. 35); a subsidy roll showing William
Shakespeare as a defaulter in respect of a tax of five shillings,
October, 1596, and of thirteen shillings and four pence, October, 1598, based on an assessment made about 1593 or 1594,
when the poet was living in St. Helen's, Bishopsgate, and
paid after he had moved to Southwark (*Athenæum*, March 16,
1906, and L. 42); Royal Warrant for a Patent and the Patent

itself (May 19, 1603) licensing the company of actors, "Laurence Fletcher, William Shakespeare, Richard Burbage, Augustine Phillippes, John Hemmings, Henrie Condell, William Sly, Robert Armyn, Richard Cowly and the rest of their associates" as the King's Servants (L. 87, 88); the Accounts of the Revels at Court in the reigns of Elizabeth and James, containing entries showing performances at Court of "The Moor of Venis," "The Merry Wives of Winsor," "Mesur for Mesur" by "Shaxberd," "the plaie of Errors" by "Shaxberd," "Loves Labours lost," "Henry the fift," and "the Martchant of Venis" by "Shaxberd" (twice, being "againe commanded by the Kings Matie"), all in 1604 (O.S.), of "the Tempest" and "ye winters nightes Tayle" in 1611, all by the King's men, and of the performance before the Court at Wilton, Dec. 2, 1603 (L. 96, 133, *Notes in the History of the Revels Office under the Tudors,* ed. by E. K. Chambers, and *Supposed Shakespeare Forgeries,* by Ernest Law); record of the purchase in 1610 of an estate in Old Stratford and Stratford-on-Avon by Shakespeare from William and John Combe (L. 127); three documents in a Chancery suit relating to the ownership of property in Blackfriars, April 26, May 15, May 22, 1615 (C. W. Wallace in *Englische Studien,* April, 1906, and Preface to New Edition of Lee's *Life,* xxii ff.); the grant for cloaks for the King's entry into London, March 15, 1604 (Ld. Chamberlain's Papers, No. 600); the documents in the law suit among the heirs of Richard Burbage (1635), relating to the ownership of the Globe and the Blackfriars theaters, and giving much information on the value of theatrical shares, actors' salaries, etc. (H.-P. i. 312–319); and the documents in the lawsuit of Bellots *vs.* Mountjoy (1612), including Shakespeare's deposition (*New Shakespeare Discoveries,* C. W. Wallace, *Harper's Magazine,* March, 1910).

4

THE SHAKESPEARE'S BIRTHPLACE MUSEUM IN STRATFORD-ON-AVON contains several documents of importance: record of the conveyance in 1602 of an estate in Old Stratford from William and John Combe to William Shakespeare (L. 79, H.-P. II, 17–19); extract from the Court Rolls of the Manor of Rowington, transferring from Walter Getley to William Shakespeare certain premises in Chapel Lane, Stratford-on-Avon (L. 81); the conveyance to Shakespeare from Ralph Hubande of the residue of a lease of a moiety of the tithes of Stratford-on-Avon, Old Stratford, Welcombe, and Bishopton (L. 99); the diary of one Thomas Greene, containing a reference to the dispute as to the inclosing of common lands (reproduced in facsimile in C. M. Ingleby's *Shakespeare and the Enclosure of Common Fields at Welcombe, 1885*).

5

THE BRITISH MUSEUM possesses the Ms. diary of John Manningham of the Middle Temple, which, under the date of Feb. 2, 1601, records a performance of *Twelfth Night*, and the anecdote recorded above, p. 44 (L. 77; Ms. Harl. 5353, ed. Camden Soc., p. 39); also the Mortgage Deed from Shakespeare to Henry Walker on the property in Blackfriars conveyed to Shakespeare and others on the day previous, March 10, 1612/13.

6

THE BODLEIAN LIBRARY AT OXFORD has the Ms. diary of Dr. Simon Forman describing performances of *Winter's Tale*, *Cymbeline*, and *Macbeth* in 1610 and 1611 (L. 128; Ms. Ashmol. 208, fol. 201b); and the Accounts of Lord Stanhope of Harrington, Treasurer of the Chamber to James I, containing the following entry: "1613, May 20. Item paid to John

Heminges uppon the cowncells warrant dated att Whitehall
xx⁰ die Maii 1613 for presentinge before the Princes highnes
the La : Elizabeth and the Prince Pallatyne Elector fowerteene
severall playes viz . . .   Much adoe abowte nothinge . . .
The Tempest . . .   The Winters Tale, Sʳ John Falstafe,
The Moore of Venice . . . Cæsars Tragedye . . . All wᶜʰ
Playes weare played within the tyme of this Accompte, viz
pᵈ the some of iiij. (xx.) xiij.li. vj.s. viij.d.

"Item paid to the said John Heminges uppon the lyke
warrant dated att Whitehall xx⁰ die Maij 1613 for presenting
sixe severall playes viz. one playe called . . .   And one other
called Benidicte and Betteris all played within the tyme of
this Accompte viz pᵈ ffortie powndes And by waye of his
Maᵗˡˢ rewarde twentie powndes In all . . . lx li." (L. 138;
Ms. Rawl. A. 239).

7

The Episcopal Register of the Diocese of Worcester
contains the bond given by Sandells and others for the marriage of Shakespeare and Anne Hathaway (L. 12).

8

The Library of the Guildhall in London has the in-
denture prepared for the purchaser in the sale of the house in
Blackfriars on March 10, 1613, by Henry Walker to William
Shakespeare and others (L. 136). The indenture held by the
seller is in the library of Mr. Marsden J. Perry, Providence,
R. I.

9

The Principal Probate Registry, Somerset House,
London, contains Shakespeare's Will, which runs as follows:

[1] VICESIMO quinto die [Januarii] *Martii*, anno regni domini nostri Jacobi, nunc regis Angliæ, &c., decimo quarto, et Scotiæ xlix°, annoque Domini 1616.

— T. WMI. SHACKSPEARE

In the name of God, Amen! I William Shackspeare, of Stratford upon Avon in the countie of Warr., gent., in perfect health and memorie, God be praysed, doe make and ordayne this my last will and testament in manner and forme followeing, that ys to saye, ffirst, I comend my soule into the handes of God my Creator, hoping and assuredlie beleeving, through thonelie merittes, of Jesus Christe my Saviour, to be made partaker of lyfe everlastinge, and my bodye to the earth whereof yt ys made. Item, I gyve and bequeath unto my [sonne and] [2] daughter Judyth one hundred and fyftie poundes of lawfull English money, to be paied unto her in the manner and forme foloweng, that ys to saye, one hundred poundes *in discharge of her marriage porcion* within one yeare after my deceas, with consideracion after the rate of twoe shillinges in the pound for soe long tyme as the same shalbe unpaied unto her after my deceas, and the fyftie poundes residwe thereof upon her surrendring *of*, or gyving of such sufficient securitie as the overseers of this my will shall like of, to surrender or graunte all her estate and right that shall discend or come unto her after my deceas, or *that shee* nowe hath, of, in, or to, one copiehold tenemente, with thappurtenaunces, lyeing and being in Stratford upon Avon aforesaied in the saied countye of Warr., being parcell or holden of the mannour of Rowington, unto my daughter Susanna Hall and her heires for ever. Item, I

---

[1] The words which have been erased are put between brackets; those which have been interlined are printed in italics.

[2] So Lambert. Halliwell-Phillipps reads "sonne in L."

gyveand bequeath unto my saied daughterJudith one hundred
and fyftie poundes more, if shee or anie issue of her bodie be
lyvinge att thend of three yeares next ensueing the daie of the
date of this my will, during which tyme my executours are
to paie her consideracion from my deceas according to the
rate aforesaied ; and if she dye within the saied tearme without issue of her bodye, then my will ys, and I doe gyve and
bequeath one hundred poundes thereof to my neece Elizabeth
Hall, and the fiftie poundes to be sett fourth by my executours
during the lief of my sister Johane Harte, and the use and
proffitt thereof cominge shalbe payed to my saied sister Jone,
and after her deceas the saied $1.^{li.}$ shall remaine amongst the
children of my saied sister, equallie to be divided amongst
them ; but if my saied daughter Judith be lyving att thend
of the saied three yeares, or anie yssue of her bodye, then my
will ys, and soe I devise and bequeath the saied hundred and
fyftie poundes to be sett out *by my executours and overseers*
for the best benefitt of her and her issue, and *the stock* not *to
be* paied unto her soe long as she shalbe marryed and covert
baron [by my executours and overseers] ; but my will ys, that
she shall have the consideracion yearelie paied unto her
during her lief, and, after her deceas, the saied stock and
consideracion to bee paied to her children, if she have anie,
and if not, to her executours or assignes, she lyving the saied
terme after my deceas. Provided that yf suche husbond as
she shall att thend of the saied three years be marryed unto,
or att anie after (*sic*) doe sufficientlie assure unto her and
thissue of her bodie landes awnswereable to the porcion by this
my will gyven unto her, and to be adjudged soe by my executours and overseers, then my will ys, that the said $cl.^{li.}$ shalbe
paied to such husbond as shall make such assurance, to his
owne use. Item, I gyve and bequeath unto my saied sister

P

Jone xx.^li. and all my wearing apparrell, to be paied and delivered within one yeare after my deceas; and I doe will and
devise unto her *the house* with thappurtenaunces in Stratford,
wherein she dwelleth, for her naturall lief, under the yearlie
rent of xij.^d. Item, I gyve and bequeath unto her three sonnes,
William Harte, . . . Hart, and Michaell Harte, fyve pounds
a peece, to be paied within one yeare after my deceas [to be
sett out for her within one yeare after my deceas by my executours, with thadvise and direccions of my overseers, for her
best profitt, untill her mariage, and then the same with the
increase thereof to be paied unto her]. Item, I gyve and
bequeath unto [her] *the saied Elizabeth Hall*, all my plate,
except my brod silver and gilt bole, that I now have att the
date of this my will. Item, I gyve and bequeath unto the
poore of Stratford aforesaied tenn poundes; to Mr. Thomas
Combe my sword; to Thomas Russell esquier fyve poundes;
and to Frauncis Collins, of the borough of Warr. in the countie
of Warr. gentleman, thirteene poundes, sixe shillinges, and
eight pence, to be paied within one yeare after my deceas.
Item, I gyve and bequeath to [Mr. Richard Tyler thelder]
Hamlett Sadler xxvj.^s. viij.^d. to buy him a ringe; to *William
Raynoldes gent., xxvj.^s. viij.^d. to buy him a ringe;* to my godson
William Walker xx^s. in gold; to Anthonye Nashe gent., xxvj.^s.
viij.^d.; and to Mr. John Nashe xxvj.^s. viij.^d. [in gold]; *and to
my fellowes John Hemynges, Richard Burbage, and Henry Cun-
dell, xxvj.^s. viij.^d. a peece to buy them ringes.* Item, I gyve, will,
bequeath, and devise, unto my daughter Susanna Hall, *for
better enabling of her to performe this my will, and towards the
performans thereof*, all that capitall messuage or tenemente
with thappurtenaunces, *in Stratford aforesaid*, called the New
Place, wherein I nowe dwell, and two messuages or tenementes
with thappurtenaunces, scituat, lyeing, and being in Henley

streete, within the borough of Stratford aforesaied; and all
my barnes, stables, orchardes, gardens, landes, tenementes,
and hereditamentes, whatsoever, scituat, lyeing, and being,
or to be had, receyved, perceyved, or taken, within the townes,
hamletes, villages, fieldes, and groundes, of Stratford upon
Avon, Oldstratford, Bushopton, and Welcombe, or in anie of
them in the saied countie of Warr. And alsoe all that messuage or tenemente with thappurtenaunces, wherein one John
Robinson dwelleth, scituat, lyeing and being, in the Black-
friers in London, nere the Wardrobe; and all my other landes,
tenementes, and hereditamentes whatsoever, To have and to
hold all and singuler the saied premisses, with theire appur-
tenaunces, unto the saied Susanna Hall, for and during the
terme of her naturall lief, and after her deceas, to the first
sonne of her bodie lawfullie yssueing, and to the heires males
of the bodie of the saied first sonne lawfullie yssueinge; and
for defalt of such issue, to the second sonne of her bodie, lawfullie issueinge, and [of] to the heires males of the bodie of the
saied second sonne lawfullie yssueinge; and for defalt of such
heires, to the third sonne of the bodie of the saied Susanna
lawfullie yssueing, and of the heires males of the bodie of the
saied third sonne lawfullie yssueing; and for defalt of such
issue, the same soe to be and remaine to the ffourth [sonne],
ffyfth, sixte, and seaventh sonnes of her bodie lawfullie issue-
ing, one after another, and to the heires males of the bodies
of the saied fourth, fifth, sixte, and seaventh sonnes lawfullie
yssueing, in such manner as yt ys before lymitted to be and
remaine to the first, second, and third sonns of her bodie, and
to theire heires males; and for defalt of such issue, the said
premisses to be and remaine to my sayed neece Hall, and the
heires males of her bodie lawfullie yssueinge; and for defalt
of such issue, to my daughter Judith, and the heires males of

her bodie lawfullie issueinge; and for defalt of such issue, to the right heires of me the saied William Shakspeare for ever. *Item, I gyve unto my wief my second best bed with the furniture.* Item, I gyve and bequeath to my saied daughter Judith my broad silver gilt bole. All the rest of my goodes, chattels, leases, plate, jewels, and household stuffe whatsoever, after my dettes and legasies paied, and my funerall expenses dischardged, I give, devise, and bequeath to my sonne in lawe, John Hall gent., and my daughter Susanna, his wief, whom I ordaine and make executours of this my last will and testament. And I doe intreat and appoint *the saied* Thomas Russell esquier and Frauncis Collins gent. to be overseers hereof, and doe revoke all former wills, and publishe this to be my last will and testament. In witness whereof I have hereunto put my [seale] *hand*, the daie and yeare first abovewritten.

By me WILLIAM SHAKSPEARE.

Witnes to the publyshing hereof,

FRA: COLLYNS,[1]
JULYUS SHAWE,
JOHN ROBINSON,
HAMNET SADLER,
ROBERT WHATTCOTT.

Probatum coram magistro Willielmo Byrde, legum doctore comiss. &c. xxij^do. die mensis Junii anno Domini 1616, juramento Johannis Hall, unius executorum, &c. cui &c. de bene &c. jurat. reservat. potestate &c. Susannæ Hall, alteri executorum &c. cum venerit petitur, &c. (Inv. ex.)

[1] Francis Collyns was the lawyer at Warwick who prepared the will, of which the draft only was executed, no time being possible for an engrossed copy. — Note by Lambert.

10

THE HERALDS' COLLEGE has the two drafts of a grant of arms to John Shakespeare in 1596 (Ms. Vincent. Coll. Arm. 157, arts. 23, 24); and the confirmation of the grant in 1599 (L. 30, 55). For further details on the matter of the coat of arms, see *Herald and Genealogist*, i. 510, and for facsimiles, *Miscellanea Genealogica et Heraldica*, 2d ser. 1886, i. 109. On the criticism of the herald's complaisance in the matter of the Shakespeare and similar grants, see Preface to New Edition (1909) of Lee's *Life*, pp. xi-xv.

11

THE STATIONERS' REGISTER, accessible in the *Transcript* edited by E. Arber, 5 vols. 1875–94, contains the records of the entries of those of Shakespeare's works which were registered either with or without his name. The Shakespearean entries are gathered out of the great mass contained in these volumes by Lambert, Fleay, Stokes, H. P., *Chronological Order of Shakespeare's Plays*, 1878, Appendix V, and others.

12. MISCELLANEOUS

The literary allusions to Shakespeare in the sixteenth and earlier seventeenth centuries have been collected in *Shakespeare's Century of Praise*, revised and reëdited by J. Munro as *The Shakespeare Allusion Books*, London, 1909.

Greene's attack in *Greenes Groatsworth* will be found in its context in his works, ed. A. B. Grosart, 1881–1886, and Chettle's Apology in his *Kind Hartes Dreame*, Percy Society, 1874.

The Historical MSS. Commission's Report on the Historical MSS. of Belvoir Castle, IV. 494, contains the entry from the Belvoir Household Book as to Rutland's "impresa." See also

Times, December 27, 1905, and Preface to New Edition of Lee's *Life*, pp. xvi–xxii.

13. EXTRACTS FROM MERES'S *PALLADIS TAMIA*, 1598

As the Greeke tongue is made famous and eloquent by *Homer*, *Hesiod*, *Euripedes*, *Æschilus*, *Sophocles*, *Pindarus*, *Phocylides* and *Aristophanes;* and the Latine tongue by *Virgill*, *Ovid*, *Horace*, *Silius Italicus*, *Lucanus*, *Lucretius*, *Ausonius* and *Claudianus:* so the English tongue is mightily enriched, and gorgeouslie invested in rare ornaments and resplendent abiliments by sir *Philip Sidney*, *Spencer*, *Daniel*, *Drayton*, *Warner*, *Shakespeare*, *Marlow* and *Chapman*.

As the soule of *Euphorbus* was thought to live in *Pythagoras:* so the sweete wittie soule of *Ovid* lives in mellifluous & hony-tongued Shakespeare, witnes his *Venus* and *Adonis*, his *Lucrece*, his sugred Sonnets among his private friends, &c.

As *Plautus* and *Seneca* are accounted the best for Comedy and Tragedy among the Latines, so *Shakespeare* among yᵉ English is the most excellent in both kinds for the stage; for Comedy, witnes his *Gētlemē of Verona*, his *Errors*, his *Love labors lost*, his *Love labours wonne*, his *Midsummers night dreame*, & his *Merchant of Venice:* for Tragedy, his *Richard the 2*, *Richard the 3*, *Henry the 4*, *King Iohn*, *Titus Andronicus*, and his *Romeo* and *Iuliet*.

As *Epius Stolo* said, that the Muses would speake with *Plautus* tongue, if they would speak Latin: so I say that the Muses would speak with *Shakespeares* fine filed phrase, if they would speake English.

As *Ovid* saith of his worke:

> Iamque opus exegi, quod nec Iovis ira, nec ignis,
> Nec poterit ferrum, nec edax abolere vetustas.

And as *Horace* saith of his; *Exegi monumentum ære peren-nius; Regalique; situ pyramidum altius; Quod non imber edax; Non Aquilo impotens possit diruere; aut innumerabilis annorum feries &c fuga temporum:* so say I severally of sir *Philip Sidneys, Spencers, Daniels, Draytons, Shakespeares,* and *Warners workes;*

As *Pindarus, Anacreon* and *Callimachus* among the Greekes; and *Horace* and *Catullus* among the Latines are the best Lyrick Poets: so in this faculty the best among our Poets are *Spencer* (who excelleth in all kinds) *Daniel, Drayton, Shakespeare, Bretton.*

As . . . so these are our best for Tragedie, the Lorde *Buckhurst,* Doctor *Leg* of Cambridge, Doctor *Edes* of Oxforde, maister *Edward Ferris,* the Authour of the *Mirrour for Magistrates, Marlow, Peele, Watson, Kid, Shakespeare, Drayton, Chapman, Decker,* and *Benjamin Johnson.*

. . . so the best for Comedy amongst us bee, *Edward* Earle of Oxforde, Doctor *Gager* of Oxford, Maister *Rowley* once a rare Scholler of learned Pembroke Hall in Cambridge, Maister *Edwardes* one of her Maiesties Chappell, eloquent and wittie *John Lilly, Lodge, Gascoyne, Greene, Shakespeare, Thomas Nash, Thomas Heywood, Anthony Mundye* our best plotter, *Chapman, Porter, Wilson, Hathway,* and *Henry Chettle.*

. . . so these are the most passionate among us to bewaile and bemoane the perplexities of Love, *Henrie Howard* Earle of Surrey, sir *Thomas Wyat* the elder, sir *Francis Brian,* sir *Philip Sidney,* sir *Walter Rawley,* sir *Edward Dyer, Spencer, Daniel, Drayton, Shakespeare, Whetstone, Gascoyne, Samuell Page* sometimes fellowe of *Corpus Christi* Colledge in Oxford, *Churchyard, Bretton.*

14. THE INSCRIPTION ON SHAKESPEARE'S MONUMENT IN
THE CHURCH OF THE HOLY TRINITY, STRATFORD-ON-AVON

Judicio Pylium, genio Socratem, arte Maronem
Terra tegit, populus mæret, Olympus habet.

Stay, passenger, why goest thou by so fast?
Read, if thou canst, whom envious death hath plast
Within this monument: Shakespeare with whome
Quick nature dide; whose name doth deck ys tombe
Far more than cost; sith all yt he hath writt
Leaves living art but page to serve his witt.

Obiit ano. doi 1616. Ætatis 53.   Die 23 Ap.

15. THE INTRODUCTORY MATTER IN THE FIRST FOLIO

TO THE MOST NOBLE

AND

INCOMPARABLE PAIRE OF BRETHREN.

WILLIAM

Earle of Pembroke, &c.   Lord Chamberlaine to the
Kings most Excellent Maiesty.

AND

PHILIP

Earle of Montgomery, &c. Gentleman of his Maiesties Bed-
Chamber.

Both Knights of the most Noble Order of the Garter,
and our singular good LORDS.

Right Honourable,

WHILST we studie to be thankful in our particular, for the
many fauors we haue receiued from your L. L. we are falne
vpon the ill fortune, to mingle two the most diuerse things
that can bee, feare, and rashnesse; rashnesse in the enter-
prize, and feare of the successe. For, when we valew the

places your H. H. sustaine, we cannot but know their dignity greater, then to descend to the reading of these trifles: and, while we name them trifles, we haue depriu'd our selues of the defence of our Dedication. But since your L. L. haue beene pleas'd to thinke these trifles some-thing, heeretofore; and haue prosequuted both them, and their Authour liuing, with so much fauour: we hope, that (they out-liuing him, and he not hauing the fate, common with some, to be exequutor to his owne writings) you will vse the like indulgence toward them, you haue done vnto their parent. There is a great difference, whether any Booke choose his Patrones, or finde them: This hath done both. For, so much were your L. L. likings of the seuerall parts, when they were acted, as before they were published, the Volume ask'd to be yours. We haue but collected them, and done an office to the dead, to procure his Orphanes, Guardians: without ambition either of selfe-profit, or fame: onely to keepe the memory of so worthy a Friend, & Fellow aliue, as was our SHAKESPEARE, by humble offer of his playes, to your most noble patronage. Wherein, as we haue iustly obserued, no man to come neere your L. L. but with a kind of religious addresse; it hath bin the height of our care, who are the Presenters, to make the present worthy of your H. H. by the perfection. But, there we must also craue our abilities to be considerd, my Lords. We cannot go beyond our owne powers. Country hands reach foorth milke, creame, fruites, or what they haue: and many Nations (we haue heard) that had not gummes & incense, obtained their requests with a leauened Cake. It was no fault to ap-proch their Gods, by what meanes they could: And the most, though meanest, of things are made more precious, when they are dedicated to Temples. In that name therefore, we most humbly consecrate to your H. H. these remaines of your seruant SHAKESPEARE; that what delight is in them, may be euer your L. L. the reputation his, & the faults ours, if any be committed, by a payre so carefull to shew their gratitude both to the liuing, and the dead, as is

Your Lordshippes most bounden,
IOHN HEMINGE.
HENRY CONDELL.

To the Great Variety of Readers. — From the most able to him that can but spell; — there you are number'd. We had rather you were weighd, especially when the fate of all bookes depends upon your capacities, and not of your heads alone, but of your purses. Well! It is now publique, and you will stand for your privileges wee know; to read and censure. Do so, but buy it first. That doth best commend a booke, the stationer saies. Then, how odde soever your braines be, or your wisedomes, make your licence the same and spare not. Judge your sixe-pen'orth, your shillings worth, your five shillings worth at a time, or higher, so you rise to the just rates, and welcome. But, whatever you do, buy. Censure will not drive a trade or make the jacke go. And though you be a magistrate of wit, and sit on the stage at Black-Friers or the Cock-pit to arraigne playes dailie, know, these playes have had their triall alreadie, and stood out all appeales, and do now come forth quitted rather by a Decree of Court than any purchas'd letters of commendation.

It had bene a thing, we confesse, worthie to have bene wished, that the author himselfe had liv'd to have set forth and overseen his owne writings; but since it hath bin ordain'd otherwise, and he by death departed from that right, we pray you do not envie his friends the office of their care and paine to have collected and publish'd them; and so to have pub-

lish'd them, as where (before) you were abus'd with diverse
stolne and surreptitious copies, maimed and deformed by the
frauds and stealthes of injurious impostors that expos'd
them; even those are now offer'd to your view cur'd and
perfect of their limbes, and all the rest absolute in their num-
bers as he conceived them; who, as he was a happie imitator
of Nature, was a most gentle expresser of it. His mind and
hand went together; and what he thought, he uttered with
that easinesse that wee have scarse received from him a blot in
his papers. But it is not our province, who onely gather his
works and give them you, to praise him. It is yours that
reade him. And there we hope, to your divers capacities,
you will finde enough both to draw and hold you; for his wit
can no more lie hid then it could be lost. Reade him, therefore; and againe and againe; and if then you doe not like
him, surely you are in some manifest danger not to understand him. And so we leave you to other of his friends, whom,
if you need, can bee your guides. If you neede them not,
you can leade yourselves and others; and such readers we
wish him. — *Iohn Heminge.* — *Henrie Condell.*

TO THE MEMORY OF MY BELOUED,

THE AVTHOR

MR. WILLIAM SHAKESPEARE:
AND
what he hath left vs.

To draw no enuy (*Shakespeare*) on thy name,
   Am I thus ample to thy Booke, and Fame:
While I confesse thy writings to be such,
   As neither *Man*, nor *Muse,* can praise too much.

'Tis true, and all mens suffrage.   But these wayes
   Were not the paths I meant vnto thy praise:
For seeliest Ignorance on these may light,
   Which, when it sounds at best, but eccho's right;
Or blinde Affection, which doth ne're aduance
   The truth, but gropes, and vrgeth all by chance;
Or crafty Malice, might pretend this praise,
   And thinke to ruine, where it seem'd to raise.
These are, as some infamous Baud, or Whore,
   Should praise a Matron.   What could hurt her more?
But thou art proofe against them, and indeed
   Aboue th' ill fortune of them, or the need.
I, therefore will begin.   Soule of the Age!
   The applause! delight! the wonder of our Stage!
My *Shakespeare*, rise; I will not lodge thee by
   Chaucer, or *Spenser*, or bid *Beaumont* lye
A little further, to make thee a roome:
   Thou art a Moniment, without a tombe,
And art aliue still, while thy Booke doth liue,
   And we haue wits to read, and praise to giue.
That I not mixe thee so, my braine excuses;
   I meane with great, but disproportion'd *Muses:*
For, if I thought my iudgement were of yeeres,
   I should commit thee surely with thy peeres,
And tell, how farre thou didstst our *Lily* out-shine,
   Or sporting *Kid*, or *Marlowes* mighty line.
And though thou hadst small *Latine*, and lesse *Greeke*,
   From thence to honour thee, I would not seeke
For names; but call forth thund'ring *Æschilus*,
   Euripides, and *Sophocles* to vs,
Paccuuius, Accius, him of *Cordoua* dead,
   To life againe, to heare thy Buskin tread,

And shake a Stage: Or, when thy Sockes were on,
　　Leaue thee alone, for the comparison
Of all, that insolent *Greece*, or haughtie *Rome*
　　Sent forth, or since did from their ashes come.
Triumph, my *Britaine*, thou hast one to showe,
　　To whom all Scenes of *Europe* homage owe.
He was not of an age, but for all time!
　　And all the *Muses* still were in their prime,
When like *Apollo* he came forth to warme
　　Our eares, or like a *Mercury* to charme!
Nature her selfe was proud of his designes,
　　And ioy'd to weare the dressing of his lines!
Which were so richly spun, and wouen so fit,
　　As, since, she will vouchsafe no other Wit.
The merry *Greeke*, tart *Aristophanes*,
　　Neat *Terence*, witty *Plautus*, now not please;
But antiquated, and deserted lye
　　As they were not of Natures family.
Yet must I not giue Nature all: Thy Art,
　　My gentle *Shakespeare*, must enioy a part.
For though the *Poets* matter, Nature be,
　　His Art doth giue the fashion.　And, that he,
Who casts to write a liuing line, must sweat,
　　(Such as thine are) and strike the second heat
Vpon the *Muses* anuile: turne the same,
　　(And himselfe with it) that he thinkes to frame;
Or for the lawrell, he may gaine a scorne,
　　For a good *Poet's* made, as well as borne.
And such wert thou.　Looke how the fathers face
　　Liues in his issue, euen so, the race
Of *Shakespeares* minde, and manners brightly shines
　　In his well torned, and true-filed lines:

In each of which, he seemes to shake a Lance,
  As brandish't at the eyes of Ignorance.
Sweet Swan of *Auon!* what a sight it were
  To see thee in our waters yet appeare,
And make those flights vpon the bankes of *Thames*,
  That so did take *Eliza*, and our *Iames!*
But stay, I see thee in the *Hemisphere*
  Aduanc'd, and made a Constellation there!
Shine forth, thou Starre of *Poets*, and with rage,
  Or influence, chide, or cheere the drooping Stage;
Which, since thy flight fro hence, hath mourn'd like night,
  And despaires day, but for thy Volumes light.

BEN: IONSON.

VPON THE LINES AND LIFE OF THE FAMOUS

Scenicke Poet, Master WILLIAM SHAKESPEARE

THOSE hands, which you so clapt, go now, and wring
You *Britaines* braue; for done are *Shakespeares* dayes:
His dayes are done, that made the dainty Playes,
Which made the Globe of heau'n and earth to ring.
Dry'de is that veine, dry'd is the *Thespian* Spring,
Turn'd all to teares, and *Phœbus* clouds his rayes:
That corp's, that coffin now besticke those bayes,
Which crown'd him *Poet* first, then *Poets* King.
If *Tragedies* might any *Prologue* haue,
All those he made, would scarse make one to this:
Where *Fame*, now that he gone is to the graue
(Deaths publique tyring-house) the *Nuncius* is.
    For though his line of life went soone about,
    The life yet of his lines shall neuer out.

HVGH HOLLAND.

TO THE MEMORIE

of the deceased Authour Maister

W. SHAKESPEARE

Shake-speare, at length thy pious fellowes giue
The world thy Workes: thy Workes, by which, out-liue
Thy Tombe, thy name must: when that stone is rent,
And Time dissolues thy *Stratford* Moniment,
Here we aliue shall view thee still.   This Booke,
When Brasse and Marble fade, shall make thee looke
Fresh to all Ages: when Posteritie
Shall loath what's new, thinke all is prodegie
That is not *Shake-speares* eu'ry Line, each Verse
Here shall reuiue, redeeme thee from thy Herse.
Nor Fire, nor cankring Age, as *Naso* said,
Of his, thy wit-fraught Booke shall once inuade.
Nor shall I e're beleeue, or thinke thee dead
(Though mist) vntill our bankrout Stage be sped
(Jmpossible) with some new straine t'out-do
Passions of *Iuliet*, and her *Romeo;*
Or till J heare a Scene more nobly take,
Then when thy half-Sword parlying *Romans* spake.
Till these, till any of thy Volumes rest
Shall with more fire, more feeling be exprest,
Be sure, our *Shake-speare*, thou canst neuer dye,
But crown'd with Lawrell, liue eternally.

L. DIGGES.

To the memorie of M. *W. Shake-speare.*

WEE wondred (*Shake-speare*) that thou went'st so soone
From the Worlds-Stage, to the Graues-Tyring-roome.
Wee thought thee dead, but this thy printed worth,
Tels thy Spectators, that thou went'st but forth

To enter with applause.   An Actors Art,
Can dye, and liue, to acte a second part.
That's but an *Exit* of Mortalitie;
This, a Re-entrance to a Plaudite.   I. M.

*The Workes of William Shakespeare, containing all his
Comedies, Histories, and Tragedies; truely set forth according
to their first Originall.* — *The names of the Principall Actors in
all these playes.* — William Shakespeare; Richard Burbadge;
John Hemmings; Augustine Phillips; William Kempt;
Thomas Poope; George Bryan; Henry Condell; William
Slye; Richard Cowly; John Lowine; Samuell Crosse; Alex-
ander Cooke; Samuel Gilburne; Robert Armin; William
Ostler; Nathan Field; John Underwood; Nicholas Tooley;
William Ecclestone; Joseph Taylor; Robert Benfeld; Robert
Goughe; Richard Robinson; John Shancke; John Rice.

*A Catalogue of the severall Comedies, Histories, and Tragedies
contained in this Volume.* — COMEDIES. The Tempest,
folio 1; The Two Gentlemen of Verona, 20; The Merry Wives
of Windsor, 38; Measure for Measure, 61; The Comedy of
Errours, 85; Much adoo about Nothing, 101; Loves Labour
lost, 122; Midsommer Nights Dreame, 145; The Merchant
of Venice, 163; As You Like it, 185; The Taming of the
Shrew, 208; All is well that Ends well, 230; Twelfe-Night,
or what you will, 255; The Winters Tale, 304. — HISTORIES.
The Life and Death of King John, fol. 1; The Life and Death
of Richard the Second, 23; The First Part of King Henry the
Fourth, 46; The Second Part of K. Henry the fourth, 74;
The Life of King Henry the Fift, 69; The First part of King
Henry the Sixt, 96; The Second part of King Hen. the Sixt,
120; The Third part of King Henry the Sixt, 147; The Life
and Death of Richard the Third, 173; The Life of King

Henry the Eight, 205. — TRAGEDIES. The Tragedy of Coriolanus, fol. 1; Titus Andronicus, 31; Romeo and Juliet, 53; Timon of Athens, 80; The Life and death of Julius Cæsar, 109; The Tragedy of Macbeth, 131; The Tragedy of Hamlet, 152; King Lear, 283; Othello, the Moore of Venice, 310; Anthony and Cleopater, 346; Cymbeline King of Britaine, 369.

II. SOURCES OF TRADITIONAL MATERIAL

Fuller's Worthies of England. 1662.

Aubrey's Lives of Eminent Men, 2 vols. Ed. A. Clark, Oxford, 1895.

Diary of Rev. John Ward (1661–1663). Ed. C. A. Severn, 1839.

Rev. William Fulman's and Rev. Richard Davies's Mss. Corpus Christi College, Oxford.

John Dowdall's Travels in Warwickshire (1693). London, 1838.

William Hall (1694), Letter in Bodleian Mss. London, 1884.

William Oldys, Ms. Adversaria in British Museum, printed in Appendix to Yeowell's Memoir of Oldys, 1862.

Archdeacon Plume's Ms. memoranda at Maldon, Essex. See Lee, *Nineteenth Century*, May, 1906, and Preface to New Edition (1909) of *Life*.

For the anecdote of the Bidford Drinkers, see H.-P. and Greene's Legend of the Crab Tree, 1857.

Antony Wood. Athenæ Oxonienses, 1692.

Appendix B

Doctor, English. Mcb. IV. iii.
Doctor, Scotch. Mcb. V. i.
Dogberry. MAdo. III. iii.
Dolabella. A&C. III. xii.
Doll Tearsheet. 2H4. II. iv.
Don Adriano de Armado. LLL. I. ii.
Donalbain. Mcb. II. iii.
Don John. MAdo. I. i.
Don Pedro. MAdo. I. i.
Dorcas. WT. IV. iv.
Dorset, Marquis of. R3. I. iii.
Douglas, Archibald, Earl of. 1H4. IV. i.
Drawers. 2H4. II. iv.
Dromio of Ephesus. CofE. I. ii.
Dromio of Syracuse. CofE. I. ii.
Duke, in banishment. AYLI. II. i.
Duke Frederick. AYLI. I. ii.
Duke of Milan. TGV. II. iv.
Dull. LLL. I. i.
Dumain. LLL. I. i.
Duncan, King. Mcb. I. ii.

Edgar. Lear I. ii.
Edmund. Lear I. i.
Edmund, Earl of Rutland. 3H6. I. iii.
Edward, Earl of March, later Edward IV. 3H6. I. i; R3. II. i.
Edward IV, King. 3H6. I. i; R3. II. i.
Edward V, King. R3. III. i.
Edward, Prince of Wales, afterwards Edward V. R3. III. i.
Edward Plantagenet, Prince of Wales. 3H6. I. i.
Egeus. MND. I. i.
Eglamour. TGV. IV. iii.
Egyptian. A&C. V. i.
Elbow. Meas. II. i.

Eleanor, Duchess of Gloucester. 2H6. I. ii.
Eleanor, Queen. John I. i.
Elizabeth, Queen (as L. Grey). 3H6. III. ii; R3. I. iii.
Ely, Bishop of. H5. I. i.
Ely, Bishop of. R3. III. iv.
Emilia. Oth. II. ii.
Emilia. WT. II. ii.
Enobarbus. A&C. I. ii.
Eros. A&C. III. v.
Erpingham, Sir Thomas. H5. IV. i.
Escalus, Prince. R&J. I. i.
Escalus. Meas. I. i.
Escanes. Per. II. iv.
Essex, Earl of. John I. i.
Euphronius. A&C. III. xii.
Evans, Sir Hugh. MWW. I. i
Executioners. John IV. i.
Exeter (Beaufort), Duke of. H5. I. ii; 1H6. I. i.
Exeter, Duke of. 3H6. I. i.
Exton, Sir Pierce of. R2. V. iv.

Fabian. TwN. II. v.
Fairies. MND. II. i; MWW. V. iv.
Falstaff, Sir John. 1H4. I. ii; 2H4. I. ii; MWW. I. i.
Fang. 2H4. II. i.
Fastolfe, Sir John. 1H6. III. ii.
Father that hath killed his son. 3H6. II. v.
Faulconbridge, Lady. John I. i.
Faulconbridge, Philip the Bastard. John I. i.
Faulconbridge, Robert. John I. i.
Feeble. 2H4. III. ii.
Fenton. MWW. I. iv.
Ferdinand. Tmp. I. ii.

Lion. MND. V. i.
Longaville. LLL. I. i.
Lords: AWEW. I. ii, III. i;
AYLI. II. i; Cor. V. vi;
Cym. I. ii; Hml. V. ii;
LLL. II. i; Mcb. III. iv;
Per. I. ii; R3. V. iii; TofS.
Ind.; Tim. I. i; WT. II. ii.
Lorenzo. Merch. I. i.
Lovel, Lord. R3. III. iv.
Lovell, Sir Thomas. H8. I. iii.
Luce. CofE. III. i.
Lucentio. TofS. I. i.
Lucetta. TGV. I. ii.
Luciana. CofE. II. i.
Lucianus. Hml. III. ii.
Lucilius. JC. IV. ii.
Lucilius. Tim. I. i.
Lucio. Meas. I. ii.
Lucius, Caius. Cym. III. i.
Lucius. JC. II. i.
Lucius. TA. I. i.
Lucius, young. TA. III. ii.
Lucius. Tim. III. ii; ser-
vant. Tim. III. iv.
Lucullus. Tim. III. i.
Lucy, Sir William. 1H6. IV.
iii.
Ludovico. Oth. IV. i.
Lychorida. Per. III. i.
Lymoges, Duke of Austria.
John II. i.
Lysander. MND. I. i.
Lysimachus. Per. IV. vi.

Macbeth. Mcb. I. iii.
Macbeth, Lady. Mcb. I. v.
Macduff. Mcb. II. iii.
Macduff, Lady. Mcb. IV. ii.
Macduff's son. Mcb. IV. ii.
Macmorris. H5. III. ii.
Mæcenas. A&C. II. ii.
Malcolm. Mcb. I. ii.
Malvolio. TwN. I. v.
Mamillius. WT. I. ii.

Marcellus. Hml. I. i.
Marcus Andronicus. TA. I. i.
Marcus Antonius (Antony).
JC. I. ii; A&C. I. i.
Mardian. A&C. I. v.
Margarelon. T&C. V. vi.
Margaret. MAdo. II. i.
Margaret, Queen. 1H6. V.
iii; 2H6. I. i; 3H6. I. i;
R3. I. iii.
Margaret Plantagenet, daugh-
ter of Clarence. R3. II. ii.
Maria. LLL. II. i.
Maria. TwN. I. iii.
Mariana. AWEW. III. v.
Mariana. Meas. IV. i.
Marina. Per. IV. i.
Mariner. WT. III. iii; Tmp.
I. i.
Marshal. Per. II. iii.
Marshal, Lord. R2. I. iii.
Martext, Sir Oliver. AYLI.
III. iii.
Martius. TA. I. i.
Marullus. JC. I. i.
Master. 2H6. IV. i.
Master gunner. 1H6. I. iv.
Master, of a ship. Tmp. I. i;
2H6. IV. i.
Master's Mate. 2H6. IV. i.
Mayor of London. 1H6. III.
i; R3. III. i.
Mayor of St. Alban's. 2H6.
II. i.
Mayor of York. 3H6. IV. vii.
Melun. John V. iv.
Menas. A&C. II. i.
Menecrates. A&C. II. i.
Menelaus. T&C. I. iii.
Menenius Agrippa. Cor. I. i.
Menteith. Mcb. V. ii.
Mercade. LLL. V. ii.
Merchants: CofE. I. ii; Tim.
I. i.
Mercutio. R&J. I. iv.

Oliver. AYLI. I. i.
Oliver Martext, Sir. AYLI. III. iii.
Olivia. TwN. I. v.
Ophelia. Hml. I. iii.
Orlando. AYLI. I. i.
Orleans, bastard of. 1H6. I. ii.
Orleans, Duke of. H5. III. vii.
Orsino, Duke of Illyria. TwN. I. i.
Osric. Hml. V. ii.
Ostler. 1H4. II. i.
Oswald. Lear I. iii.
Othello. Oth. I. ii.
Outlaws. TGV. IV. i.
Overdone, Mrs. Meas. I. ii.
Oxford, Earl of. 3H6. III. iii.
Oxford, Earl of. R3. V. ii.

Page. MWW. I. i.
Page, Mistress. MWW. II. i.
Page, Mistress Anne, a daughter. MWW. I. i.
Page, William, a son. MWW. IV. i.
Pages: AWEW. I. i; AYLI. V. iii; 2H4. I. ii; H8. V. i; R3. IV. ii; R&J. V. ii; Tim. II. ii. *See* Boys.
Painter. Tim. I. i.
Pandar. Per. IV. ii.
Pandarus. T&C. I. i.
Pandulph, Cardinal. John III. i.
Panthino. TGV. I. iii.
Paris. R&J. I. ii.
Paris. T&C. II. ii.
Parolles. AWEW. I. i.
Patience. H8. IV. ii.
Patrician. Cor. III. i.
Patroclus. T&C. II. i.
Paulina. WT. II. ii.
Peaseblossom. MND. III. i.

Pedant. TofS. IV. ii.
Pedro, Don. MAdo. I. i.
Pembroke, Earl of. 3H6. IV. i.
Pembroke, Earl of. John IV. ii.
Percy, Henry, Earl of Northumberland. 1H4. I. iii; 2H4. I. i; R2. III. i.
Percy, Henry (Hotspur). 1H4. I. iii; R2. II. iii.
Percy, Lady (wife of Hotspur). 1H4. II. iii; 2H4. II. iii.
Percy, Thomas, Earl of Worcester. 1H4. I. iii.
Perdita. WT. IV. iv.
Pericles. Per. I. i.
Peter. 2H6. I. iii.
Peter. R&J. II. iv.
Peter of Pomfret. John IV. ii.
Petitioners. 2H6. I. iii.
Peto. 1H4. II. ii; 2H4. II. iv.
Petruchio. TofS. I. i.
Phebe. AYLI. III. v.
Philario. Cym. I. iv.
Philemon. Per. III. ii.
Philip, King of France. John II. i.
Philo. A&C. I. i.
Philostrate. MND. V. i.
Philotus. Tim. III. iv.
Phrynia. Tim. IV. iii.
Physicians: Cym. I. v; Lear IV. iv; Mcb. IV. iii.
Pierce, Sir, of Exton. R2. V. iv.
Pinch. CofE. IV. iv.
Pindarus. JC. IV. ii.
Pirates. Per. IV. i.
Pisanio. Cym. I. i.
Pistol. 2H4. II. iv; H5. II. i; MWW. I. i.
Plantagenet. *See* Richard.
Player King. Hml. III. ii.

Rousillon, Count. *See* Bertram.
Rousillon, Countess. AWEW. I. i.
Rugby, John. MWW. I. iv.
Rumour. 2H4. Ind.
Rutland, Edmund, Earl of. 3H6. I. iii.

Sailors : Hml. IV. vi; Oth. I. iii; Per. III. i.
Salanio. Merch. I. i.
Salarino. Merch. I. i.
Salerio. Merch. III. ii.
Salisbury, Earl of. H5. IV. iii; 1H6. I. iv.
Salisbury, Earl of. 2H6. I. i.
Salisbury, Earl of. John III. i.
Salisbury, Earl of. R2. II. iv.
Sampson. R&J. I. i.
Sandys, William (Lord). H8. I. iii.
Saturninus. TA. I. i.
Say, Lord. 2H6. IV. iv.
Scales, Lord. 2H6. IV. v.
Scarus. A&C. III. x.
Scout. 1H6. V. ii.
Scribe. H8. II. iv.
Scrivener. R3. III. vi.
Scroop, Lord. H5. II. ii.
Scroop, Richard, Archbishop of York. 1H4. IV. iv; 2H4. I. iii.
Scroop, Sir Stephen. R2. III. ii.
Sea-Captain (Lieut.). 2H6. IV. i; TwN. I. ii.
Sebastian. Tmp. I. i.
Sebastian. TwN. II. i.
Secretary. H8. I i.
Seleucus. A&C. V. ii.
Sempronius. TA.*
Sempronius. Tim. III. iii.
Senators, Roman. Cor. I. i; Cym. III. vii; Venetian.

Oth. I. iii; Athenian. Tim. II. i; Coriolanian. Cor. I. ii.
Sentinels. 1H6. II. i.
Sentry. A&C. IV. ix.
Sergeant. 1H6. II. i; (at arms) H8. I. i.
Servants : A&C. II. vii; Hml. IV. vi; 1H4. II. iii; 2H4. I. ii; H8. I. iv; JC. II. ii; Lear III. vii; Mcb. III. i; Meas. II. ii; Merch. III. i; Per. III. ii; R2. II. ii; TofS. IV. i; Tim. I. ii; T&C. III. i; TwN. III. iv; WT. II. iii.
Servilius. Tim. III. ii.
Servingmen : Cor. IV. v; 1H6. I. iii; 2H6. II. iv; Merch. I. ii; TofS. Ind.
Seyton. Mcb. V. iii.
Sexton. MAdo. I. i.
Sextus Pompeius. A&C. II. i.
Shadow. 2H4. III. ii.
Shallow, Justice. 2H4. III. ii; MWW. I. i.
Shepherd. 1H6. V. iv.
Shepherd, Old. WT. III. iii.
Sheriff. 1H4. II. iv; 2H6. II. iv; R3. V. i.
Shrewsbury, Talbot, Earl of. 1H6. I. iv.
Shylock. Merch. I. iii.
Sicilius Leonatus, a ghost. Cym. V. iv.
Sicinius Velutus. Cor. I. i.
Silence. 2H4. III. ii.
Silius. A&C. III. i.
Silvia. TGV. II. i.
Silvius. AYLI. II. iv.
Simonides, King of Pentapolis. Per. II. ii.
Simpcox. 2H6. II. i.
Simpcox's wife. 2H6. II. i.
Simple, Peter. MWW. I. i.

Appendix C

R 241

Appendix D

BIBLIOGRAPHY

THIS Bibliography is arranged in divisions corresponding to the chapters of this volume. It aims to include those books most important for the student, and to furnish guidance for those interested in more specialized fields of study.

The following are the chief general bibliographies:

Shakespeare Bibliography, by William Jaggard, Stratford-on-Avon, 1911. This is useful but often inaccurate.

Shakespeare Bibliography, by Walther Ebisch and L. L. Shücking, Oxford Press, 1931.

Catalogue of the Barton Collection of the Boston Public Library, part i, Shakespeare's Works and Shakesperiana, 1878–1888. Excellent up to the date of its publication.

Jahrbuch der deutschen Shakespeare-Gesellschaft. Weimar, 1865–. The bibliographies, with indexes, issued in this annual are excellent but were much curtailed during and for some years after the War.

The Cambridge History of English Literature, vol. v, chaps. viii–xii, 1910. Good selected bibliographies.

A complete annual bibliography for all languages by Dr. S. A. Tannenbaum is issued in the Bulletin of the Shakespeare Association of America. See also The Annual Bibliography Eng. Lang. and Lit. of the Modern Humanities Research Ass'n, and The Year's Work in English Studies of the English Ass'n for current literature.

Full and serviceable bibliographical aids are to be found in Sir Edmund K. Chambers's William Shakespeare, 2 vols., 1930, and in his The Elizabethan Stage, 4 vols., 1923. For a brief selected list, see A Shakespeare Reference Library by Sir Sidney Lee and Sir Edmund K. Chambers, 1925.

CHAPTER I

Shakespeare's England and London

See bibliographies in the Cambridge Modern History, vol. iii, chap. x, and the Cambridge History of English Literature, vol. v, chap. xiv. The two most accessible and important works on the subject are: William Harrison's *Description of Britaine and England*, in Holinshed's Chronicle, 1577, reprinted in the Shaks. Soc. Publ. 1877–1888, in the Scott Library, 1899, and in Everyman's Library; and John Stow's *Survey of London*, 1st ed., 1598, reprinted in Everyman's Library. The standard modern work is *Shakespeare's England*, an account of the life and manners of his age. 2 vols., 1916. J. D. Wilson's *Life in Shakespeare's England* (Cambridge, 1911) is an excellent anthology drawn from Elizabethan publications.

The following list includes only more important and more recent books.

Aiken, L. Memoirs of the Court of James I. 2d ed., 1822.

Ashton, J. Humour, Wit, and Society in the Seventeenth Century. 1883.

Besant, Sir W. London in the Time of the Tudors. 1904.

Creizenach, W. Geschichte des neueren Dramas, Halle, 1893. See vol. iv, part i, book iii, Religios-sittliche und politisch-soziale Anschauungen der Theaterdichter.

Cheyney, E. P. A History of England from the Defeat of the Armada to the Death of Elizabeth. 2 vols. 1913, 1926.

Douce, F. Illustrations of Shakespeare and of Ancient Manners. 1839.

An English Garner. New ed., 1903. See vols.: Social

England Illustrated; Tudor Tracts, 1532–1582; Stuart Tracts, 1603–1693.

Froude, J. A. History of England from the Fall of Wolsey to the Defeat of the Armada. 1856–1870. Reprinted in Everyman's Library.

Gildersleeve, V. Government Regulation of the Elizabethan Drama. New York, 1908.

Hall, H. Society in the Elizabethan Age. 4th ed., 1901.

Harrison, G. B. England in Shakespeare's Day. 1927.

Jusserand, J. J. Histoire litteraire du peuple Anglais. Paris, 1904. English trans., 1909. See especially vol. ii, book v, chap. i.

Lee, S. Stratford-on-Avon from the Earliest Times to the Death of Shakespeare. 1907.

Nicholls, J. The Progresses and Processions of Queen Elizabeth. New ed., 3 vols., 1823.

—— The Progresses, Processions, and Festivities of King James I. 4 vols., 1828.

Stephenson, H. T. Shakespeare's London. New York, 1905.

—— The Elizabethan People. New York, 1910.

Strutt, J. Sports and Pastimes of the People of England. 1801. New ed., 1903.

Thompson, E. N. S. The Controversy between the Puritans and the Stage. Yale Studies in English, vol. xx. New York, 1903.

Traill, H. D. Social England. 3d ed., 1904. See vols. iii and iv.

Wheatley, H. B. London Past and Present. 3 vols., 1891.

CHAPTER II

Biographical Facts and Traditions

Adams, J. Q. A Life of William Shakespeare. 1923.

Chambers, Sir Edmund K. William Shakespeare, a study of facts and problems. 2 vols., 1930. Vol. II gives a full collection of documents.

Halliwell-Phillipps, J. O. Outlines of the Life of Shakespeare. 2 vols. 7th ed., 1887. Later eds. are reprints. With illustrations, facsimiles, and a full collection of documents.

Lambert, D. H. Shakespeare Documents. (Published originally as Cartæ Shakespeareanæ, 1904.) A chronological catalogue of extant evidence.

Lee, Sidney. A Life of William Shakespeare. London and New York, 1898. New and revised eds., 1909, 1916.

—— Shakespeare in Oral Tradition, Chap. III in Shakespeare and the Modern Stage, 1906.

The preceding are the most important books, but the following are useful in various ways: Shakespeare of Stratford. C. F. Tucker Brooke. 1926. A Chronicle History of the Life and works of Shakspere. F. G. Fleay. London, 1886. Shakespeare's Marriage. J. W. Gray. 1905. Shakespeare's Family. C. C. Stopes. 1901. Shakespeare's Warwickshire Contemporaries. C. C. Stopes. 1907. Shakespeare's Environment. C. C. Stopes. 1914. The Life of Henry, Third Earl of Southampton. C. C. Stopes. 1922. New Shakespeare Discoveries. C. W. Wallace. Harper's Magazine, March, 1910. Master Richard Quyny. E. I. Fripp. 1924. Shakespeare's Stratford, 1928, Shakespeare Studies, 1930. E. I. Fripp. Was Shakspere a Gentleman? S. A. Tannen-

baum. 1909. Catalogues of the books, manuscripts, works
of art, antiquities, and relics at present exhibited in Shakespeare's birthplace, Stratford-on-Avon, 1910, 1916, 1925.
For discussion of portraits of Shakespeare, see Portraits of
Shakespeare, J. P. Norris, Philadelphia, 1885; M. R. Spiel-
mann in Stratford-Town Shakespeare, vol. x; and in Studies
in the First Folio, 1925, article on Shakespeare's Portraiture.
On autographs and handwriting see Sir E. M. Thompson,
Shakespeare's Handwriting, 1916; S. A. Tannenbaum, Problems in Shakspere's Penmanship, 1927; The Handwriting
of the Renaissance, 1930; and W. W. Greg, English Literary
Autographs. 1925, 1928.

See also Sources of Traditional Material, Appendix A, p. 225.

CHAPTER III

Shakespeare's Reading

Shakespeare's Books: A dissertation on Shakespeare's reading and the immediate sources of his works. By H. R. D. Anders. Berlin, 1904. The best book on the subject.

Shakespeare's Studies. T. S. Baynes, 1893.

Shakespeare's Holinshed. Ed. W. G. Boswell-Stone. 1896. New ed., 1907. A reprint of the passages in Holinshed's Chronicles which Shakespeare used.

Shakespeare's Plutarch. Ed. W. W. Skeat. 1875.

Mr. William Shakespeare. Henrietta C. Bartlett. 1917. This gives a bibliography of source books.

The Shakespeare Classics, gen. ed. L. Gollancz (in progress, 1907–), reprints the chief sources of the plays: Lodge's Rosalynde, Greene's Pandosto, Brooke's Romeus and Juliet, the Chronicle History of King Leir, The Taming of a Shrew, The Sources and Analogues of A Mid-summer-Night's Dream, Shakespeare's Plutarch. Most of these, with other valuable material, are found also in W. C. Hazlitt's revision of Collier's Shakespeare Library. 6 vols. 1875 (out of print).

Many translations which Shakespeare may have known are included in the long series of the Tudor Translations, ed. W. E. Henley and Charles Whibley (mostly out of print).

For drama see Bibliography, chap. vi; for contemporary literature see bibliography in Cambridge History of English Literature; or any short manual, as Saintsbury's Elizabethan Literature, or Seccombe and Allen's Age of Shakespeare. 2 vols.

CHAPTER IV

CHRONOLOGY AND DEVELOPMENT

The first thorough attempt to determine the chronology of Shakespeare's plays was made in Malone's "Attempt to ascertain the order in which the plays attributed to Shakespeare were written," published in Steevens's edition of 1778. His final conclusions on the subject are to be found in the preliminary volumes of the 1821 Variorum. Since then, discussions of chronology and development have appeared in almost every edition of Shakespeare's Works and in many volumes discussing his life and art. (See Bibliography for Chaps. II and VIII.) The following are the most important contributions to the general question of the chronology.

Hertzberg, W. G. Preface to Cymbeline in Ulrici's ed. of Schlegel and Tieck's trans. of Shakespeare, 1871.

—— Metrisches, grammatisches, chronologisches zu Shakespeares Dramen. Jahrbuch, xiii, 1878.

Fleay, F. G. Shakspere Manual, 1878.

New Shakspere Society. Publications for 1874 contain Fleay's tests as originally proposed with discussions by Furnivall, Ingram, et al. Publications for 1877–9 contain F. S. Pulling's essay on The Speech-ending test, p. 457.

Ingram, J. K. On the weak endings of Shakspere with some account of the verse-tests in general. N. S. S. Publ. 1874.

König, G. Der Vers in Shaksperes Dramen. Quellen und Forschungen, vol. 61, 1888. The fullest presentation of numerical results for various verse tests.

Furnivall, F. J. Preface to the Leopold Shakespeare, 1876.

Hales, J. W. The Succession of Shakespeare's plays. 1874.

Ingleby, C. M. Shakespeare, the Man and the Book. 1881. Part II contains Fleay's corrected tables.

CHAPTER V

The Elizabethan Drama

Full bibliographies of both plays and critical works are to be found in Schelling's Elizabethan Drama, in the Cambridge History of English Literature, vols. v and vi, and in E. K. Chambers's Elizabethan Stage.

1. EDITIONS OF PLAYS

Convenient collections, often with valuable introductions and notes, are: Dodsley's Old English Plays, ed. W. C. Hazlitt, 15 vols., 1874–1876; Manly's Pre-Shaksperean Drama, 2 vols., Boston; Neilson's Chief Elizabethan Dramatists, Boston, 1911 (30 plays in one volume); the Mermaid Series of the Old Dramatists (4 or 5 plays by one author in each vol.); the Belles Lettres Edition (with excellent bibliographies), Boston; Masterpieces of the English Drama, New York; Temple Dramatists. Valuable reprints of old plays and documents are found in the following series now in progress: The Tudor Facsimile Texts, ed. J. S. Farmer, 43 vols., 1907; Materialien zur Kunde des älteren englischen Dramas, ed. W. Bang, Louvain, 1902; Publications of the Malone Society, 1906.

Collected editions of the chief dramatists include those of Greene, Peele, Webster, Ford, Beaumont and Fletcher, and Shirley, ed. by Alexander Dyce; of Middleton, Marston, Marlowe, and Webster, by A. H. Bullen, and the more recent editions from the Clarendon Press, — Greene, ed. J. Churton Collins; Kyd, by F. S. Boas; Lyly, by W. Bond; Nash, by R. B. McKerrow; Marlowe, by C. F. Tucker Brooke; Jonson (in progress) by C. H. Herford and P. Simpson. There are also recent editions of Beaumont and Fletcher by A. R. Waller, Cambridge, and of Chapman by T. Parrott.

2. CRITICAL AND HISTORICAL

Die Geschichte des neueren Dramas. W. Creizenach (5 vols.). Halle, 1893–1916. This is the standard history of the modern drama; vol. iv dealing with the Shakespearean period has been translated into English.

History of English Dramatic Literature to the Death of Queen Anne. A. W. Ward. 2d ed. 3 vols. 1899.

Elizabethan Drama. F. E. Schelling. 2 vols. Boston, 1902. This contains valuable bibliographies and a finding list for the plays.

The Mediæval Stage. E. K. Chambers. 2 vols. Oxford, 1903. Authoritative for the pre-Elizabethan drama, with valuable bibliography and appendices.

A Bibliographical Chronicle of the English Drama, 1559–1642. F. G. Fleay. A work of great value to scholars, but not of much service to the general reader.

The Elizabethan Stage. E. K. Chambers. 4 vols. 1923. This is the latest and most authoritative reference book.

The Cambridge History of English Literature. Vols. 4 and 5.

Other works less comprehensive in scope, but dealing with special aspects or divisions of the drama, are: Tragedy, A. H. Thorndike, Boston, 1908; English Comedy, A. H. Thorndike, 1929; Shakespeare and his Predecessors, F. S. Boas, 1896; Tudor Drama, C. F. Tucker Brooke, Boston, 1912; University Drama in the Tudor Age, F. S. Boas, 1914; Elizabethan Playwrights, F. E. Schelling, 1925.

Special treatises which have also been drawn upon for this chapter are: F. E. Schelling's English Chronicle Play, New York, 1902; A. H. Thorndike's Influence of Beaumont and

Fletcher on Shakspere, 1901; and Hamlet and the Revenge Plays, Publ. Mod. Lang. Assn., 1902; E. E. Stoll's John Webster, 1905; F. H. Ristine's English Tragi-Comedy, 1910; Reyher's Les Masques Anglais, Paris, 1909; W. W. Greg's Pastoral Poetry and Pastoral Drama, 1906; C. W. Wallace's The Evolution of the English Drama, 1912; A. W. Reed's Early Tudor Drama, 1926; C. M. Gayley's Representative English Comedies, 3 vols., 1903–14.

CHAPTER VI

The Elizabethan Theater

Sir E. K. Chambers's *The Elizabethan Stage*, 4 vols., 1923, is the standard authority with full bibliographies. A. H. Thorndike's *Shakespeare's Theater*, 1916, is briefer but comprehensive. Greg's admirable edition of Henslowe's Diary, Fleay's researches, and Murray's supplements to them are all valuable for students.

Adams, J. Q. Shakespearean Playhouses. 1917.

Albright, V. E. The Shakespearian Stage. New York, 1909.

Baldwin, T. W. The Organization and Personnel of the Shakespearean Company. 1927.

Braines, W. W. The Site of the Globe Playhouse. 1921.

Campbell, L. B. Scenes and Machines on the English Stage during the Renaissance. 1923.

Collier, J. P. Memoirs of the Principal Actors in the Plays of Shakespeare. Shaks. Soc., 1846.

Feuillerat, A. Documents relating to the Office of the Revels in the time of Queen Elizabeth. Louvain, 1908.

Fleay, F. G. A Chronicle History of the London Stage. 1890.

—— A Biographical Chronicle of the English Drama, 1559–1642. 2 vols., 1891.

Gildersleeve, V. Government Regulation of the Elizabethan Theater. New York, 1908.

Graves, T. S. The Court and the London Theatres during the Reign of Elizabeth. 1913.

Greg, W. W., ed. Henslowe's Diary, 2 parts. 1907–1908.

Greg, W. W.   Henslowe Papers.   1907.

Lawrence, W. J.   The Elizabethan Playhouse and other studies.   Stratford.   Two Series, 1912, 1913.

Mantzius, R.   A History of Theatrical Art in Ancient and Modern Times.   1904.   Cf. vol. iii.

Murray, J. T.   English Dramatic Companies, 1558–1642. 1910.

Reynolds, G. F.   Some Principles of Elizabethan Staging. Reprinted from Modern Philology.   Chicago, 1905.

—— What we know of the Elizabethan Stage, Modern Philology, July, 1911.   With bibliography of recent discussions.

Withington, R.   English Pageantry.   2 vols., 1918, 1920.

CHAPTER VII

HISTORY OF THE TEXT

1. COMPLETE EDITIONS

In one volume.

The Globe Edition, ed. W. G. Clark and W. Aldis Wright. 1864.

The ' Oxford ' Edition, ed. W. J. Craig. Oxford, 1904.

The ' Cambridge Poets ' Edition, ed. with introductions to each play, ed. W. A. Neilson. Boston, 1906 (the text used in the Tudor Shakespeare).

Annotated Library Editions.

The Cambridge Shakespeare, ed. W. Aldis Wright. 9 vols. 1863–1866. 2d ed., 1891–1893. The text known as the Cambridge text is very near to that of the Globe ed., and these have been generally used in recent editions.

A new Variorum Edition, ed. H. Howard Furness and H. H. Furness, Jr. (in progress). Philadelphia, 1871. This ed. prints (latterly) the First Folio text with exhaustive variants and annotations. The appendices supply much illustrative matter.

The Arden Shakespeare, general ed. W. J. Craig, 1899. Publ. in the U. S. without special title by Bobbs-Merrill Co., Indianapolis.

The Eversley Edition, ed. by C. H. Herford. 10 vols., 1901–1907.

The Tudor Shakespeare, general editors W. A. Neilson and A. H. Thorndike. 39 vols. The Macmillan Co. 1913.

Among other modern editions are the Rolfe, 40 vols., 1871, revised 1896; Temple, ed. I. Gollancz, 40 vols., 1894,

1895; the Yale, 1917–   ; the new Cambridge, ed. by Sir A. Quiller-Couch and J. D. Wilson.   1921–   .

Historical Editions.

The most valuable is the Third Variorum, Boswell and Malone, 21 vols., 1821.   The other principal editions are discussed in this volume, and include: Rowe, 1709, 1714; Pope, 1723–1725; Theobald, 1733; Hanmer, 1744; Warburton, 1747; Johnson, 1765; Steevens (20 plays), 1766; Capell, 1768; Steevens (and Johnson), 1773; Malone, 1790; Reed (Steevens and Johnson), 1st Variorum, 1803; 2d Variorum, 1813; Knight, 1838–1842, second ed., 1842–1844; Hudson, 1851–1856; Delius, 1854–1861; Dyce, 1857, second ed., 1864–1867; White, 1857–1860, second ed., 1859–1865.

2. FACSIMILE REPRINTS

The First Folio.   With introd. by Sidney Lee.   Oxford, 1902.

The First, Second, Third, and Fourth Folios.   Methuen, 1904–1910.

The First Folio, reprint, L. Booth, 1869.

The First Folio, in reduced facsimile, J. O. Halliwell-Phillipps, 1876.   Very small type.

Quarto Facsimiles.   E. W. Ashbee.   48 vols.   1862–1871.

Quarto Facsimiles reproduced by photographic process, J. W. Griggs, under the superintendence of F. J. Furnivall. 43 vols.   1883–1889.

Shakespeare's Poems and Pericles, with introduction by Sidney Lee.   5 vols.   Oxford, 1905.

3. CONDITIONS OF PUBLICATION

Albright, E. M. Dramatic Publication in England, 1580–1640. 1927.

Bartlett, Henrietta C. Mr. William Shakespeare. 1917.

Bartlett, Henrietta C. and Pollard, A. W. A Census of Shakespeare's Plays in Quarto, 1594–1709. 1916.

Pollard, A. W. Shakespeare's Folios and Quartos. 1909.

—— Shakespeare's Fight with the Pirates. 1917, 1920.

—— The Foundation of Shakespeare's Text. 1923.

Simpson, P. Shakespearean Punctuation. 1911.

Studies in the First Folio. Intro. by Sir I. Gollancz. Oxford. 1925.

See also E. K. Chambers, William Shakespeare, for discussion and bibliography.

4. GLOSSARIES, GRAMMARS, ETC.

The standard concordance is Bartlett's *New and Complete Concordance*, 1894. The standard dictionary and one of the great monuments of Shakespeare scholarship is Alexander Schmidt's *Shakespeare-Lexikon*. 2 vols. Berlin, 1894, 1895. 3d ed., 1902. This contains valuable appendices on syntax. The most recent brief glossary is C. T. Onion's *Shakespeare Glossary*. Oxford, 1911. It makes partial use of the valuable material in the New English Dictionary. The best grammar in English, though now somewhat out of date, is F. A. Abbott's *Shakespearian Grammar*, 1869, often reprinted.

The following are also of value:

Cunliffe, R. J. A New Shakespearean Dictionary. 1910.

Dyce, A. A Glossary to the Works of Shakespeare. 1867. Revised by H. Littledale, 1902.

Ellis, A. J.   On Early English Pronunciation, with especial reference to Shakspere and Chaucer.   5 parts.   E. E. T. S., 1869–1889.

Foster, J.   A Shakespeare Word-Book.   1908.

Franz, W.   Shakespeare-Grammatik.   2 parts.   Halle, 1898–1900.   3rd ed., 1924.   No English translation.

Skeat, W. W. and Mayhew, A. L.   A Glossary of Tudor and Stuart Words.   1914.

Stokes, F. P.   A Dictionary of Characters and Proper Names.   1924.

Sugden, E. H.   A Topographical Dictionary to the Works of Shakespeare and His Fellow Dramatists.   Manchester, 1925.

Vietor, W.   A Shakespeare Phonology.   Marburg and London, 1906.

CHAPTER VIII

QUESTIONS OF AUTHENTICITY

1. THE DOUBTFUL PLAYS

The Shakespeare Apocrypha. Ed. C. F. T. Brooke. Oxford, 1908. This contains texts of fourteen of the plays discussed in this chapter.

The Two Noble Kinsmen. Ed. H. Littledale. New Shaks. Soc. Publ., 1876.

The Double Falsehood. Ed. W. H. Graham. With discussion of its relation to Cardenio. Cleveland, O. 1920.

Robertson, J. M. The Shakespeare Canon. 1922.

Pollard, A. W. et al. Shakespeare's Hand in the Play of Sir Thomas More. 1923.

Tannenbaum, S. A. The Booke of Sir Thomas Moore. 1927. This and the preceding book will furnish sufficient guidance for the controversy over this play; but see also Tannenbaum's Problems in Shakspere's Penmanship, 1927.

2. FORGERIES

Ingleby, C. M. The Shakespeare Fabrications. 1859. A complete review of the Collier forgeries, with bibliography.

Ireland, W. H. Confessions containing the particulars of his fabrication of the Shakespeare manuscripts. 1808.

Malone, E. Inquiry into the Authenticity (of the Ireland Ms.). 1796.

Law, E. Some Supposed Shakespeare Forgeries. 1911.

Tannenbaum, S. A. Shakspere Forgeries in the Revels Accounts. 1928.

Wheatley, H. B. Notes on the life of John Payne Collier. 1884. Gives a list and account of the spurious documents.

3. THE BACON CONTROVERSY

Allen, C. Notes on the Bacon-Shakespeare question. Boston, 1900. An account of Shakespeare's legal phrases.

Bacon, Delia. The Philosophy of the Plays of Shakespeare Unfolded. 1857.

Beeching, H. C. William Shakespeare: Player, Playmaker and Poet. A reply to Mr. George Greenwood. 1908.

Bompas, G. C. The Problem of Shakespeare's Plays. 1902.

Booth, W. S. Some Acrostic Signatures of Francis Bacon. Boston, 1909.

Connes, Georges. Le Mystère Shakespearien. Paris, 1926.

Donnelly, I. The Great Cryptogram. 2 vols. Chicago, 1887.

Fiske, John. Forty Years of Bacon-Shakespeare Folly. Atlantic Monthly, 1897; reprinted in Century of Science, 1899.

Gallup, E. W. The Bi-literal Cypher of Francis Bacon.

Greenwood, G. G. The Shakespeare Problem restated. Lane, 1908.

—— In re Shakespeare Beeching v. Greenwood. Lane, 1909.

Lang, A. Shakespeare, Bacon, and the Great Unknown. 1912.

Robertson, J. M. The Baconian Heresy. 1913.

Wyman, W. H. Bibliography of the Shakespeare-Baconian controversy. Cincinnati. 1884. Continued in Shakespeariana. Philadelphia.

CHAPTER IX

Shakespeare since 1616

1. THE SEVENTEENTH AND EIGHTEENTH CENTURIES

The Shakespeare Allusion Books. Ed. J. Munro. 2 vols. This reprints references to Shakespeare before 1700.

The Praise of Shakespeare. C. E. Hughes. 1904.

Eighteenth Century Essays on Shakespeare. Ed. D. Nichol Smith. Glasgow. Contains Rowe's, Pope's, Theobald's, Johnson's prefaces, Farmer's essay on Shakespeare's learning, Morgann's essay on Falstaff, etc.

Shakespearian Wars. T. R. Lounsbury. i. Shakespeare as a Dramatic Artist. ii. Shakespeare and Voltaire. 2 vols. Yale Univ., 1901.

First Editors of Shakespeare (Pope and Theobald). T. R. Lounsbury. 1906.

Considerable matter in the following volumes from the Clarendon Press bears on the early criticism of Shakespeare: Elizabethan Critical Essays, ed. Gregory Smith, 2 vols.; Seventeenth Century Critical Essays, ed. J. E. Spingarn, 3 vols.; Dryden's Essays, ed. W. P. Ker, 2 vols. See also Eighteenth Century Essays on Shakespeare, ed. D. Nichol Smith.

2. THE NINETEENTH AND TWENTIETH CENTURIES

Baker, G. P. The Development of Shakespeare as a Dramatist. Macmillan, 1907.

Boas, F. S. Shakespeare and his Predecessors. 1895.

Bradley, A. C. Shakespearean Tragedy. Macmillan, 1904.

Bradley, A. C. Oxford Lectures on Poetry. Macmillan, 1909.

Brandes, G. William Shakespeare. Copenhagen, 1896. Eng. trans. 2 vols., 1898.

Coleridge, S. T. Notes and Lectures on Shakespeare, etc. 2 vols. 1849. Reprinted in Everyman's Library, the New Universal Library, and Bohn's Library.

Collins, J. C. Studies in Shakespeare. 1904.

Columbia University. Shakesperian Studies. 1916.

Dowden, E. Shakspeare: His Mind and Art. 1874.

―― Introduction to Shakespeare. 1893.

Elze, K. William Shakespeare. Halle, 1876. Eng. trans., 1888.

Goethe. Wilhelm Meister, book IV, chaps. 13–16, contains an analysis of Hamlet.

―― Dichtung und Wahrheit, and Eckermann's Reports of Goethe's conversations contain references. An essay "Shakespeare und kein Ende" appears in his collected works.

Hazlitt, W. Characters of Shakespeare's plays, 1817. Reprinted in Everyman's Library, New Universal Library, Bohn's Library.

Heine, Heinrich. Shakespeare's Maidens and Women, in Works. Eng. trans. Heinemann, 1851.

Jameson, Mrs. Shakespeare's Heroines. Temple Classics.

Kreyssig, F. S. T. Vorlesungen über Shakespeare. 2 vols. 3d ed. Berlin, 1876.

Lamb, Charles. On Some of the Old Actors (Essays of Elia). Reprinted in Everyman's Library.

―― On the Tragedies of Shakespeare (Misc. essays). Reprinted in Temple Classics.

Lawrence, W. W. Shakespeare's Problem Comedies. 1931.

Lee, Sidney. Shakespeare and the Modern Stage. 1906.

Lessing, G. E. Laokoön, and Dramatic Notes. Eng. trans., Bohn's Library.

MacCallum, M. W. Shakespeare's Roman Plays and their Background. 1910.

Martin, Lady (Helen Faucit). On Some of Shakespeare's Female Characters. 1885.

Masefield, J. William Shakespeare, 1911.

Matthews, Brander. Shakespeare as a Playwright. 1913.

Moulton, R. G. Shakespeare as a Dramatic Artist. Oxford, 1885.

—— The Moral System of Shakespeare. 1903.

Raleigh, W. Shakespeare (English Men of Letters). 1907.

Schlegel, A. W. von. Lectures on Dramatic Art and Literature. Reprinted in Bohn's Library.

Schücking, L. L. Die Charakter-probleme bei Shakespeare. 1919. Eng. trans., 1922.

Stoll, E. E. Shakespeare Studies. 1927.

Swinburne, A. C. A Study of Shakespeare. 1880.

Thorndike, A. H. The Influence of Beaumont and Fletcher on Shakespeare. 1901.

—— Shakespeare in America. 1927.

Tolman, A. H. Falstaff and Other Shakespearean Topics. 1925.

Wendell, B. William Shakspere. 1894.

White, R. G. Studies in Shakespeare. 9th ed. 1896.

—— Shakespeare's Scholar. 1854.

Wisconsin, University of. Shakespeare Studies. 1916.

Important critical and interpretative aids will also be found in the bibliographies for earlier chapters, as in the complete editions of Shakespeare's works, in histories of literature and the drama, or in special studies, as Anders's Shakespeare's Books, and Madden's Diary of Master William Silence.

For a handy bibliography of studies of botany, folk-lore, law, medicine, the supernatural in Shakespeare, etc., see the Cambridge History of English Literature, vol. v. pp. 450, 451, to which may be added Freytag, G., Technique of the Drama, Eng. trans. 1891; Matthews, B., A Study of the Drama, 1910; Arnold, M. E., Soliloquies of Shakespeare, New York, 1911; Fansler, H. E., Evolution of Technic in Elizabethan Tragedy, 1914; Archer, W., Play Making, 1912.

3. STAGE HISTORY

The standard work is by G. C. D. Odell, *Shakespeare from Betterton to Irving*, 2 vols., 1920. Genest's *Some Account of the English Stage from the Restoration in 1660 to 1830*, long the standard history has been supplemented and partly replaced by three volumes by A. Nicoll: *A History of Restoration Drama*, 1923; *A History of Early Eighteenth Century Drama*, 1925, and *A History of Late Eighteenth Century Drama*, 1927.

Baker, H. B.   The London Stage, 1576–1903.   1904.

Doran, J.   Their Majesties' Servants.   1888.   Ed. R. W. Lowe.

Fitzgerald, P.   A New History of the English Stage.   2 vols. London, 1882.

Hazlitt, W.   A View of the English Stage.   1818.

Horne, R. H.   New Spirit of the Age.   1884.

Lowe, R. W.   Bibliographical Account of English Dramatic Literature.   1888.

Odell, G. C. D.   Annals of the New York Stage (in progress).

Phelps, W. M., and Forbes Robertson, J.   Life and Works of Samuel Phelps.   London, 1886.

Seilheimer, G. O.   A History of the American Theater. 3 vols.   Philadelphia, 1891.

Thaler, A.   Shakspere to Sheridan.   1922.

4. SHAKESPEARE ON THE CONTINENT

A good selected bibliography is to be found in the Cambridge History of English Literature, vol. v, pp. 456–472. Only a few of the most important titles are given here, including some already noted.

Baldensperger, F. Esquisse d'une Histoire de Shakespeare en France. Paris, 1910.

Böhtling, A. R. A. Goethe und Shakespeare. Leipzig, 1909.

Burckhardt, C. A. H. Das Repertoire des Weimarischen Theaters unter Goethes Leitung. Hamburg, 1901.

Chateaubriand, F. R. de. Shakespeare. 1801.

Cohn, A. Shakespeare in Germany in the Sixteenth and Seventeenth Centuries. Berlin, 1865.

Creizenach, W. Die Schauspiele der englischen Komödianten. Stuttgart, 1889.

Delius, N. Sämmtliche Werke, Kritische Ausgabe. 1854–1861. 5th ed., 1882.

Elze, K. William Shakespeare. Halle, 1876.

Genée, R. Geschichte der Shakespeareschen Dramen in Deutschland. Leipzig, 1870.

Guizot, F. De Shakespeare et de la Poésie dramatique. Paris, 1822.

Haines, C. M. Shakespeare in France. Criticism from Voltaire to Victor Hugo. 1925.

Heine, H. Shakespeares Mädchen und Frauen, in sämmtliche Werke. vol. v, 1839. Eng. trans., 1895.

Hugo, F. V. Œuvres complètes de Shakespeare, traduites. 18 vols. Paris, 1856–1867.

Hugo, Victor. Cromwell, Preface. Paris, 1827.

—— William Shakespeare. Paris, 1864.

Jusserand, J. J. Shakespeare en France sous l'ancien régime. Paris, 1898. Eng. trans. London, 1899.

Koeppel, E. Studien über Shakespeare's Wirkung auf zeitgenössische Dramatiker. Louvain, 1905.

Kreyssig, F. Vorlesungen über Shakespeare und seine Werke. 1858. 3d ed., 1877.

Lee, Sidney. Shakespeare in France. In Shakespeare and the Modern Stage.

Lessing, G. E. Hamburgische Dramaturgie. Nos. 12, 15, 73. 1767, 1768.

Lounsbury, T. R. Shakespeare and Voltaire. 1902.

Mézières, A. Shakespeare, ses œuvres et ses critiques. Paris, 1860.

Renan, E. Caliban, Suite de la Tempête. Paris, 1878.

Schlegel, A. W. Ueber dramatische Kunst und Literatur. Heidelberg, 1809–1811.

—— Shakespeare's Dramatische Werke, übersetzt. 1797–1810. Neue Ausgabe, ergänzt und erläutert von L. Tieck. 9 vols. 1825, 1880–1883. Revised by Ulrici, 1867–1871, by Grandl, 1897–1899, by H. Conrad, 1905.

Stendhal (Henri Bergh) Racine et Shakespeare. Paris, 1823.

Taine, H. Histoire de la litterature anglaise. Paris, 1844. Eng. trans., rev. ed., 1873.

Ten Brink, B. Shakespeare. Strassburg, 1893.

Tolstoi, L. N. Shakespeare. 1906.

Ward, A. W. History of English Dramatic Literature. vol. i, pp. 534 ff.

Index